Response
to
Intervention

A Framework for Reading Educators

Douglas Fuchs, Lynn S. Fuchs, Sharon Vaughn
Editors

INTERNATIONAL
Reading Association
800 BARKSDALE ROAD, PO BOX 8139
NEWARK, DE 19714-8139, USA
www.reading.org

The International Reading Association attempts, through its publications, to provide a forum for a wide spectrum of opinions on reading. This policy permits divergent viewpoints without implying the endorsement of the Association.

Executive Editor, Books   Corinne M. Mooney
Developmental Editor   Charlene M. Nichols
Developmental Editor   Tori Mello Bachman
Developmental Editor   Stacey Lynn Sharp
Editorial Production Manager   Shannon T. Fortner
Design and Composition Manager   Anette Schuetz

Project Editors   Charlene M. Nichols and Christina Lambert

Cover   Design, Lise Holliker Dykes; Photographs (from top), iStockphoto.com, Banana Stock, Banana Stock

Library of Congress Cataloging-in-Publication Data
Response to intervention : a framework for reading educators / edited by Douglas Fuchs, Lynn S. Fuchs, and Sharon Vaughn.
    p. cm.
 Includes bibliographical references and index.
 ISBN 978-0-87207-622-8
 1. Remedial teaching. 2. Reading disability. 3. Learning disabled children--Education. I. Fuchs, Douglas. II. Fuchs, Lynn. III. Vaughn, Sharon, 1952-
 LB1029.R4R47 2008
 372.4--dc22
                                                                                    2008015429

Contents

About the Editors

Douglas Fuchs, PhD, is the Nicholas Hobbs Professor of Special Education and Human Development at Vanderbilt University, Nashville, Tennessee, where he also codirects the Kennedy Center Reading Clinic. He is the author of 225 articles in peer-reviewed journals and has won "best paper" awards for several of these publications, including the American Educational Research Association's (AERA) Palmer O. Johnson Memorial Award. In 2004, he was identified by Thompson ISI as one of 250 most highly cited researchers in the social sciences. In 2003 and 2005, respectively, he was given the Career Research Award by the Council for Exceptional Children and the Distinguished Research Award by the Special Education Research SIG of AERA. In 2005, he was a recipient of the universitywide Earl Sutherland Prize for Achievements in Research.

Photograph by Steven Green

Lynn S. Fuchs, PhD, is the Nicholas Hobbs Professor of Special Education and Human Development at Vanderbilt University, Nashville, Tennessee, where she also codirects the Kennedy Center Reading Clinic. She has conducted programmatic research on assessment methods for enhancing instructional planning and on instructional methods for improving reading and math outcomes for students with learning disabilities. She has published more than 200 empirical studies in peer-reviewed journals. She sits on the editorial boards of 10 journals including *Journal of Educational Psychology, Scientific Studies of Reading, The Elementary School Journal, Journal of Learning Disabilities*, and *Exceptional Children*. She has been identified by Thompson ISI as one of 250 most highly cited researchers in the

social sciences and has received a variety of awards to acknowledge her research accomplishments that have enhanced reading and math outcomes for children with and without disabilities. Her awards include the Council for Exceptional Children's Career Research Award, Vanderbilt University's Joe B. Wyatt Distinguished University Professor, Vanderbilt's Earl Sutherland Award for Research Accomplishments, the American Educational Research Association's (AERA) Distinguished Researcher Award from the Special Education Research SIG, and the 1998 AERA Palmer O. Johnson Award for the outstanding article appearing in an AERA-sponsored journal for the 1997 volume year.

Sharon Vaughn, PhD, is the Executive Director of the Meadows Center for Preventing Reading Difficulties and holds the H.E. Hartfelder/Southland Corporation Regents Chair in Human Development at the University of Texas, Austin. She was the Editor-in-Chief of the *Journal of Learning Disabilities* and the coeditor of *Learning Disabilities Research and Practice*. She is the recipient of the American Educational Research Association's (AERA) Special Education SIG Distinguished Researcher Award. She is the author of numerous books and research articles that address the reading and social outcomes of students with learning difficulties and disabilities, including the fourth edition of *Teaching Students Who Are Exceptional, Diverse, and At Risk in the General Education Classroom* (with Schumm & Bos; Allyn & Bacon). She is currently the principal investigator or coprincipal investigator on several Institutes for Education Science, National Institute for Child Health and Human Development, and Office of Special Education Programs research grants investigating effective interventions for students with learning disabilities and behavior problems as well as students who are English-language learners.

Contributors

Carolyn A. Denton
Associate Professor
Children's Learning Institute
Department of Pediatrics
University of Texas Health Science Center at Houston
Houston, Texas

Douglas Fuchs
Nicholas Hobbs Professor of Special Education and Human
    Development
Vanderbilt University
Nashville, Tennessee

Lynn S. Fuchs
Nicholas Hobbs Professor of Special Education and Human
    Development
Vanderbilt University
Nashville, Tennessee

Timothy Shanahan
Professor of Urban Education and Director of the UIC Center
    for Literacy
University of Illinois at Chicago
Chicago, Illinois

Pamela M. Stecker
Professor of Special Education
Eugene T. Moore School of Education
Clemson University
Clemson, South Carolina

Barbara M. Taylor

Professor of Reading Education and Director of the Minnesota Center
for Reading Research
University of Minnesota
Minneapolis, Minnesota

Sharon Vaughn

Executive Director of the Meadows Center for Preventing Reading
Difficulties and H.E. Hartfelder/Southland Corporation Regents
Chair in Human Development
University of Texas
Austin, Texas

Introduction

For the last four decades, the major approach for identifying children with learning disabilities (LD) has involved documenting a discrepancy between a child's IQ and achievement. With this discrepancy approach, identification frequently occurs after second grade. In other words, many children must "wait to fail" before they obtain the services they need. For this reason, along with various technical problems associated with discrepancy (see Vaughn & Fuchs, 2003), the 2004 reauthorization of the Individuals With Disabilities Education Improvement Act (Public Law 108–446; IDEA 2004) allows states to move from a discrepancy approach to response to intervention (RTI) for LD identification. Potential advantages of RTI include earlier identification, stronger focus on prevention, and assessment with clearer implications for academic programming (e.g., Fuchs & Fuchs, 2006; Fuchs, Fuchs, & Speece, 2002). A basic premise of RTI is that LD may be understood in terms of chronic nonresponsiveness to generally effective instruction, that such children have a disability that requires specialized treatment. Supporters of RTI believe it can help differentiate between two explanations of low achievement: inadequate instruction versus disability. If a child responds poorly to instruction that benefits most students, then this eliminates instructional quality as an explanation of poor academic growth and instead provides evidence of disability. Also, because most children respond satisfactorily to validated intervention, RTI serves an important prevention function.

Indeed, most RTI models of LD identification are conceived in good part as a multi-tier prevention system, which is also a hallmark of the federal Reading First program. Multi-tier prevention approaches are modeled after the public health care system in the United States, whereby primary care physicians address routine problems, making referrals to secondary prevention for problems that require specialized care. Tertiary intervention, which may involve short-term hospitalizations or long-term care, is reserved for the most severe and chronic illnesses.

Extending this framework to schools and reading instruction, a multi-tier prevention system typically incorporates three levels of prevention and intervention. The terms *prevention* and *intervention* refer to a continuum of services in which effective practices are implemented with early intervention supporting students who need additional instruction. The first level, or primary prevention, is general education. Students who fail to respond to this general, or "universal," curriculum enter the RTI process with additional instruction provided through secondary prevention. Secondary prevention typically involves one or more rounds of standardized, research-based small-group tutoring. Most students can be expected to respond favorably to this more intensive instruction. For this reason, the children who do not respond are thought to demonstrate "unexpected failure," and they become candidates for tertiary intervention. Tertiary intervention, the most intensive form of instruction in the RTI framework, involves individualized programming based on systematic and ongoing progress monitoring to inform instructional planning. When adequate performance is observed at this instructional level, the child returns to secondary or primary prevention. In this way, RTI has two interconnected goals: (1) to identify at-risk students early so that they may receive more intensive prevention services prior to the onset of severe deficits and disability identification and (2) to identify students with LD who are repeatedly unresponsive to validated, standardized forms of instruction and instead require individualized, data-based instruction.

Note that throughout this book, several terms are used in discussions of RTI, such as *response to instruction* and *responsiveness to instruction* as well as *response to intervention* and *responsiveness to intervention*. Terms that are associated with instruction such as *response to instruction* typically refer to instruction provided as part of the core reading program or core reading curricula. Terms that are associated with intervention such as *response to intervention* refer to how students respond to more intensive interventions such as those provided in Tier 2 and 3.

The structure of this book mirrors the framework of a multi-tier prevention system. In Chapter 1, Barbara M. Taylor describes key components of a successful primary prevention program. In Chapter 2, Lynn S. Fuchs and Douglas Fuchs present a framework for conducting RTI assessment, which is a critical component of RTI practice. RTI assessment includes procedures for screening students into secondary prevention. It also includes methods for systematically monitoring student progress to quantify student improvement, for distinguishing between adequate and inadequate response, and for inductively formulating effective individualized instructional programs. In Chapter 3, Sharon Vaughn and Carolyn A. Denton discuss various approaches for conducting secondary preventive tutoring, which are derived from extant research. In Chapter 4, Douglas Fuchs, Pamela M. Stecker, and Lynn S. Fuchs offer a conceptualization of special education as the tertiary intervention and describe essential features of a reformed special education. These features include developing data-based goals that drive instruction and the use of ongoing, empirically validated progress monitoring to help special educators inductively develop individually tailored, effective instructional programs. As proposed by Fuchs and colleagues, special education, within a multi-tier RTI prevention system, might also incorporate clear criteria for evaluating progress so that students may reenter secondary (or primary) prevention and return to tertiary intervention as needed to promote strong, long-term outcomes. Finally, in Chapter 5, Timothy Shanahan helps us understand the defining roles that make reading specialists critical for implementing RTI effectively.

The goal of this book is to provide a description of the critical features of RTI in reading and its applications in elementary grades. This book intends to provide a focus on reading educators and key stakeholders as they determine their roles and coordinate services in the response to intervention process.

REFERENCES

Fuchs, D., & Fuchs, L.S. (2006). Introduction to response to intervention: What, why, and how valid is it? *Reading Research Quarterly, 41*(1), 93–99.

Fuchs, L.S., Fuchs, D., & Speece, D.L. (2002). Treatment validity as a unifying construct for identifying learning disabilities. *Learning Disability Quarterly, 25*(1), 33–45.

Vaughn, S., & Fuchs, L.S. (2003). Redefining learning disabilities as inadequate response to instruction: The promise and potential problems. *Learning Disabilities Research and Practice, 18*(3), 137–146.

Tier 1: Effective Classroom Reading Instruction in the Elementary Grades

Barbara M. Taylor

Within the RTI framework, Tier 1 focuses on providing effective classroom reading instruction for all students. Fortunately, as educators we know a considerable amount about how to help all students in the elementary grades succeed in reading to their fullest potential. Classroom teachers providing effective classroom instruction are the key to successful outcomes for students. When classroom teachers reflect on their reading instruction as well as make good pedagogical choices from their core program and supplemental materials to meet individual students' needs, students benefit.

Throughout this chapter as I focus on sound, research-based classroom reading instruction, I cite relevant research and draw on my visits to more than 1,600 teachers' classrooms in more than 80 schools across the United States during the past 10 years. From these visits in which I gave schools feedback on their reading instruction and gained an understanding of their successes and challenges related to schoolwide reading improvement efforts, I have learned a great deal about effective reading instruction (for related research

support, see Taylor, Pearson, Peterson, & Rodriguez, 2003, 2005;
Taylor & Peterson, 2006a, 2006b, 2006c).

In this chapter, I discuss first those components of effective
reading instruction supported by scientifically based reading research
that are related to the abilities that students need to develop to
become competent readers. Because this important aspect of effective
classroom reading instruction has been extensively covered
elsewhere (National Institute of Child Health and Human
Development [NICHD], 2000; Snow, Burns, & Griffin, 1998) and
most elementary teachers have had recent professional development
on the "five dimensions of reading" under No Child Left Behind
legislation, my coverage will serve as a brief review.

Next, I discuss sound practices of teaching reading in the
classroom. In my many visits to elementary classrooms in recent
years, I have seen that this is the aspect of effective reading
instruction that teachers struggle with the most. Not only do teachers
have to skillfully orchestrate their instruction of the essential
components of reading, but also they have to do so with good
teaching practices, including appropriate pacing and clarity of
purpose tied to all students' needs and abilities.

Effective Core Reading Instruction in Grades K–5

Phonemic Awareness and Phonics Instruction

On the basis of extensive research, it is clear that most beginning
readers benefit from systematic explicit instruction in the
development of phonemic awareness and phonics knowledge
(Adams, 1990; NICHD, 2000; Snow et al., 1998; Stahl, 2001).
Kindergartners and many first-grade students profit from small-
group, explicit instruction in phonemic awareness that focuses on
learning how to hear the individual phonemes, or sounds, in words

(i.e., phonemic segmentation) and in learning how to blend phonemes together to pronounce words (i.e., phonemic blending). Having students manipulate letters while working on the auditory abilities of segmentation and blending has also been found to be beneficial (NICHD, 2000). Teaching a few important aspects

of phonemic awareness (e.g., segmentation and blending) is better than focusing on many aspects, and this teaching is most effective when it encompasses between 5 and 18 hours of total time spread out across the first year or two of school (NICHD, 2000).

Focusing on rhyme is a frequently observed phonemic awareness task in the kindergarten classes I have visited. Teachers appear to struggle more with teaching students to hear and blend the individual sounds in words. Having students write for sounds on white boards has been one effective strategy to help students develop their phonemic segmentation and blending abilities. For example, after reading a story a kindergarten teacher may ask students to listen for each of the sounds in several three-phoneme words from the story and write the letters for those sounds on their white boards.

The National Reading Panel confirmed extensive earlier research (see Adams, 1990; Ehri, 1991; Snow et al., 1998; Stahl, 2001) that children, especially in kindergarten and first grade, benefit from systematic, explicit phonics instruction. A variety of approaches are effective including synthetic (e.g., letter by letter), larger unit (e.g., onset and rime), and miscellaneous approaches (e.g., writing the sounds heard in a word). The National Reading Panel also reminded teachers that systematic phonics lessons should be integrated with other aspects of reading instruction to create a balanced reading program (NICHD, 2000, p. 2-126). In a related point, the Panel recommended that teachers help children apply their phonics knowledge accurately and fluently in their daily reading and writing activities (p. 2-135), and that children need the opportunity to read books in which newly learned phonics elements occur. Complementary research has found that teachers who see more growth in their students' reading during grades K–2 are those who are more often observed coaching (not telling) as students are trying to decode words while reading (Taylor, Pearson, Clark, & Walpole, 2000; Taylor & Peterson, 2006b, 2006c). For example, if a student were stuck on the word *nap* in a story, rather than tell the child, "The word is *nap*," the teacher might ask, "What is the short sound you just learned for *a*? Now blend the sounds for *n*, *a*, and *p* together. What is the word?" When the topic of coaching in word recognition strategies is a focus in an ongoing professional development experience, primary-grade teachers, in general, do increase the frequency with which they provide prompts and support to help students successfully decode unknown words as they are reading (Taylor & Peterson, 2006a, 2006b, 2007).

Fluency Instruction

Oral reading fluency procedures, in which students receive guidance or support, have a significant impact on students' reading (NICHD, 2000). Effective fluency procedures include a student repeatedly reading the same text while receiving feedback from a teacher or other coach and a student engaging in assisted reading of varied texts with support from a teacher or other skilled reader (Kuhn & Stahl, 2003; NICHD, 2000). However, Stahl (2004) cautioned that fluency is only one ability of a competent reader. Having students focus disproportionately on fluency to the neglect of other components of reading is not advisable. Also, Stahl found that fluency practice was most important in first and second grade, with other aspects of reading instruction gaining importance in third grade and higher.

From my current work in the primary grades, I know that fluency practice and assessment are widespread today. However, I see some teachers use fluency building programs and techniques indiscriminately—that is, with all students regardless of their fluency ability. When students can read grade-level texts at grade-level word-correct-per-minute (WCPM) targets, I question the usefulness of having these students reread a text with a focus on fluency as opposed to having them reread a text with a focus on comprehension or having them move on to the reading of a new text and new learning related to this text. Even students who would benefit from fluency practice need to be reminded to focus on reading comprehension as well as reading fluency.

> **Even students who would benefit from fluency practice need to be reminded to focus on reading comprehension.**

Vocabulary Instruction

The National Reading Panel reported that vocabulary instruction does lead to gains in reading comprehension, a finding that is not surprising given the strong relationship between vocabulary knowledge and reading comprehension ability (Nagy & Scott, 2000). The National Reading Panel and others (Baumann & Kame'enui, 2004; Blachowicz & Fisher, 2000; Graves, 2007) concluded that variety in instructional approaches is beneficial. Effective techniques include direct instruction in specific words, some prereading instruction in words, teaching of words in rich contexts, and teaching students to use strategies to determine word meanings. Students also learn words incidentally through wide reading. The Panel reported that, in general, students should study words they will find useful in many contexts. Also, repeated exposure to words in authentic contexts is helpful as is active engagement in learning words and the restructuring of vocabulary tasks when needed, especially for struggling readers.

As I visit classrooms, I am puzzled when I see a teacher who is preteaching the meanings of many words (e.g., five or more) prior to students reading the text in which these words occur. Typically when this happens, the teacher asks students what a particular word

means. The word may or may not be presented in a sentence. Someone perhaps gives a semireasonable definition of the word in question. But this seems to do little to help the others learn much about the meaning of the word because there is little or no context to help them understand it. If many such words are introduced, I see students' eyes start to glaze over as one word and its meaning becomes confused with the next word in the prereading list of words to be covered.

Beck, McKeown, and Kucan (2002) discuss the value of introducing the meanings of words that are important to comprehension as a before-reading activity if students are going to be reading a text independently. However, they suggest that the most effective place to introduce the meanings of words potentially impairing comprehension may be at the points in the text where the words occur. For example, if a teacher and the class are reading a passage about bats, and they come to the sentence, "Bats give off high-pitched sounds that help them navigate even in the dark," the teacher might stop at the end of the sentence or page and ask, "What do you think *navigate* means in this sentence?" At the end of the passage the teacher might ask students to write a sentence about or share with a friend how they navigate their way from the school bus to their classroom or how another animal, such as a dog, navigates its path while going from one place to another.

Comprehension Instruction

Comprehension, the ultimate goal of reading, is essential for lifelong learning. Skilled readers use active, strategic processes to foster good comprehension. Fortunately, instruction addressing comprehension strategies has been found to improve students' reading comprehension (NICHD, 2000; Taylor & Peterson, 2006b).

Contemporary books and articles have many suggestions about which comprehension strategies should be taught (Lipson, 2007; Pressley, 2006). Because instructional time is limited, I recommend that teachers focus on teaching strategies that have been associated with improved comprehension outcomes for students on the basis of a number of studies. The National Reading Panel concluded that explicit lessons in the following strategies were most effective: summarizing, comprehension monitoring, use of graphic and semantic organizers, use of story structure, question answering, and question generation. Cooperative learning techniques were found to benefit students as they were learning comprehension strategies. Perhaps most important, teaching students how to use multiple strategies in natural contexts, such as in small-group discussions, was found to be effective (NICHD, 2000; Pressley, 2006).

Comprehension strategy instruction is different from more traditional comprehension skill instruction and is observed in classrooms much less often (Taylor et al., 2003; Taylor & Peterson, 2006a, 2006b, 2006c). Acknowledging that different definitions of comprehension skills and strategies abound (Afflerbach, 2006), I offer one set of definitions below (Taylor et al., 2003). In my work with colleagues (Taylor et al., 2003; Taylor & Peterson, 2006a) we define traditional comprehension skill instruction as an activity in which students are asked to identify an aspect of comprehension, such as a main idea or a cause and effect, or to engage in a comprehension task when prompted, such as making a prediction or giving a retelling. With comprehension strategies instruction, the goal is to teach students one or more strategies that they ultimately will use unprompted when reading independently. Teachers need to provide explicit instruction including the following steps:

1. Explaining what the strategy is

2. Modeling or thinking aloud as they engage in the strategy

3. Coaching students as they try out the strategy themselves

4. Reminding students to use a particular strategy or set of strategies when they read

5. Getting students to use strategies independently

Comprehension strategies are difficult to teach well, perhaps in part because teachers have to talk aloud about something that they do subconsciously as skilled readers. However, with ongoing professional development, teachers can become skilled in providing effective comprehension strategies instruction that enhances students' reading abilities (Duffy et al., 1987; Garcia, Taylor, & Pearson, 2006; Pressley, 2006).

Teachers who have been provided opportunities to acquire knowledge and skills in teaching comprehension strategies instruction often implement these practices in their classroom. However, it is challenging for many teachers to seamlessly integrate important practices such as modeling, coaching, and remodeling as needed. It is also difficult to move comprehension instruction beyond talking with students about strategies to helping them actually become strategic readers as they read independently. My observations indicate that teachers who are the most successful in this task structure opportunities for students to use strategies as needed when reading and discussing text together in small groups. The teacher moves from group to group to coach them in the use of comprehension strategies and provides support and suggestions.

Teaching students how to engage in high-level talk and writing about text is another important aspect of comprehension instruction that repeatedly has been found to be related to reading gains (Guthrie et al., 2004; Guthrie, Wigfield, & Von Secker, 2000; Knapp, 1995; Lipson, 2007; Taylor et al., 2003, 2005; Taylor & Peterson, 2006a, 2006b, 2006c). Teachers see more reading growth in their students when they ask challenging questions more often, questions such as those that get students to pause and think about before answering, those that ask students to interpret a story at a high level, and those that encourage students to make connections between a text and their own experiences or with events in the world about them. Teachers ask low-level questions much more frequently than high-level questions (Taylor et al., 2003; Taylor & Peterson, 2006a, 2006b, 2006c), but with ongoing, reflective professional development, they do increase the frequency with which they engage students in high-level talk and writing about text.

Teachers who are most successful in engaging their students with high-level questioning select texts that lend themselves to high-level thinking (e.g., picture books with themes, informational books with issues, chapter books with multiple themes). Also, successful teachers teach students how to generate their own "big questions" to discuss with one another in small groups.

Looking Beyond Reading Content

Teaching effectively within the elementary classroom so that all students are reading competently to their fullest potential is a challenging endeavor that includes more than simply teaching the content of the "five components of reading." Classroom teachers need to orchestrate many different aspects of their core reading instruction and students' learning activities each day. To do this, teachers need to make good instructional choices; consider the purposes and timing of different parts of their lessons; provide students with challenging, motivating activities as they are working on their own or with other students; and have a good balance between whole-group and small-group instruction. Teachers also need to consider the balance between students' active and passive involvement in their learning

> **Teaching effectively within the elementary classroom so that all students are reading competently to their fullest potential is a challenging endeavor.**

activities as well as the balance between providing explicit, teacher–directed instruction and providing support in the form of judicious coaching as students are actively participating in literacy learning activities.

Good Instructional Choices

Within the same classroom, students are at different levels of competence related to phonemic awareness, phonics knowledge and decoding abilities, fluency, vocabulary knowledge, and comprehension abilities. Core and supplemental reading programs that teachers use contain many worthwhile instructional suggestions. However, teachers need to make good choices in the use of these materials based on students' abilities, as determined by assessment data and teaching purposes, which will vary at times for different students.

For example, it may make more sense to teach many of the recommended vocabulary words at point of contact in the story rather than prior to reading. Rereading a story as recommended for fluency practice may be less helpful for students than spending that time reading a yet unread text to learn about new ideas, information, and vocabulary. Having students do a suggested picture walk on an easy-to-understand story (e.g., a version of "City Mouse and Country Mouse" with a twist) may give the end of the story away and make the reading of the story less motivating. Having students take turns predicting what a story is going to be about from the title, as suggested in a teacher guide, may not be a good use of valuable instructional time. Asking students many of the low-level questions in a teacher's manual may not get students actively engaged in thinking about the meaning of the story whereas selecting the more challenging questions that are listed for them to respond to may lead to a spirited discussion. Calling on one student per manual-recommended stopping point (e.g., at the beginning, middle, and end and again the next day) to summarize an informational text orally may not be as effective as having students independently or with a partner write and share a summary of the text they have read after the teacher has modeled this for them.

Clarity of Purpose and Timing

An important aspect of meeting individual needs involves teaching with a clear sense of purpose. Teachers need to continually reflect on the purposes of any given lesson for the students with whom they are working—for example, teachers should ask themselves, What are the purposes of this part of my lesson? Are they the "right" purposes for the students with whom I am working? Is this part of the lesson going to move these students forward in their literacy abilities? Teachers also need to continuously reflect on the timing of different aspects of a lesson: Am I spending the right amount of time on X in this part of my lesson?

Teachers need to continually reflect on the purposes of any given lesson.

My observations reveal that instructing students on components of reading that they have already mastered, such as phonics, is not an effective use of instructional time. In my work with colleagues (Taylor et al., 2003; Taylor & Peterson, 2006c) we have reported that too much time spent on phonics for students in general in grades 2 and 3 has been found to be negatively related to students' reading growth. For example, if a group of second-grade students are already reading chapter books with high levels of accuracy, an explicit reading lesson on the sound to give er, ir, and ur when reading is probably not a good use of the students' time.

On the other hand, a phonics lesson may be appropriate for the particular students being taught, but teachers should avoid spending more time on the activity than is needed. For example, a group of second graders who are learning disabled and who are struggling with reading are likely to benefit from explicit phonics lessons (NICHD, 2000). However, having students in a single day complete multiple independent activities related to the symbol—sound correspondences for *er*, *ir*, and *ur* (e.g., worksheets, circling words with these letter combinations in text) is probably excessive, especially when compared with a variety of activities that tap into other important aspects of reading, such as reading and responding to the meanings of texts or locating and coming up with definitions of unfamiliar words in stories they have read.

Constant Use of Data

Effective teachers constantly make use of data to assess students' reading abilities and to monitor their progress. Schools have grown more sophisticated in their use of assessments to look at students' reading abilities and progress under No Child Left Behind in general, and in particular, through programs such as Reading First that require the use of such assessments. For example, in recent years I have seen widespread use of WCPM fluency measures in schools. In my many school visits, however, I see that a weak link often exists in the connection between assessment data on students' growth in reading abilities and needed changes in teaching to better meet students' needs. Teachers need to focus on questions such as the following: If a particular child is not growing as a reader, what else should I be doing? and What does this assessment data tell me about how I need to adjust my teaching for this student or group of students, whether they are below, average, or above in reading ability?

© 2008 JupiterImages Corporation

For example, if assessment data shows that in the spring of kindergarten most students know most of their letter names and consonant sounds, does it make sense to continue to drill these students on all of the symbol—sound correspondences, or does it make more sense to work in a small group with those who still need help on this? If a first grader does not yet grasp the alphabetic principle (e.g., sound out words independently) and data show the student is reading at less than 35 WCPM, does it make sense for the student to keep reading predictable books or does the student need more focused instruction on how to sound out words independently in texts that he or she cannot "read with their eyes shut"? If a second grader is reading at 90 WCPM, does it make sense for that student to first listen to a basal story being read on tape or would the student benefit more from reading the story independently?

Words-correct-per-minute assessments provide progress monitoring data on students' reading growth in the primary grades. However, these data do not provide diagnostic information. Therefore, as I visit classrooms, I am surprised that I rarely see teachers recording diagnostic information about students' reading strengths and weaknesses as they are working with students. I encourage teachers to develop a system of collecting classroom-based diagnostic information on students' reading abilities in which they rotate their focus on different students across a set period of time. For example, a teacher might take oral reading analysis notes when listening to students read in small groups or use a checklist or rubric to comment on targeted dimensions of students' comprehension abilities as he or she rotates from one small-group reading discussion to another to coach and provide feedback.

Culturally Responsive Instruction

Culturally responsive instruction in which teachers build on students' cultural strengths in the classroom is an important aspect of teaching with regard for individual differences (Au, 2006). Effective teachers have high expectations for all students and make connections between students' experiences at home and school. Effective teachers adjust their teaching practices to better accommodate students' learning styles, such as moving from a typical question–answer–question–answer session to allowing students to work together to formulate responses to questions about a text. Effective teachers also bring into their lessons literature that reflects various cultures (Au, 2006).

In the classes I visit, I am impressed with the teachers who have an extensive, multicultural literature collection available to students. Often, students in these classrooms are seen reading from this quality literature collection and enthusiastically interacting with others about these books.

Intellectual Challenge for All

As mentioned earlier, high-level thinking and intellectual challenge related to texts that are read is an important reading comprehension activity for all students and is not something that is "mastered" (Paris, 2005; Pressley, 2006; Taylor & Pearson, 2004; Taylor et al., 2003). In short, all students should be given the opportunity to engage in high-level thinking about texts at their reading level as well as with texts that the teacher reads to them or that they read in a large group lesson.

Unfortunately, in my first-year visits to schools, in many classrooms I do not see a high proportion of challenging activities that engage students in high-level thinking about texts (also see Pressley et al., 2003). To remedy this, teachers need to reflect on the questions they ask their students by asking themselves, Do I have a good balance between lower level questions that get at the facts of the story and higher level questions that get the students to think about the story? Teachers also need to reflect on the activities that students engage in while they are on their own: How am I providing students with independent activities that challenge and motivate them?

However, I am impressed when I visit a classroom, for example, in which students have to write down words they do not know the meanings of to bring to a small group, or they have to engage in high-level thinking that involves comprehension abilities such as inferencing, synthesizing, or evaluating and then write multiple sentences in a journal about what they have read. In other classrooms in which students appear to be intellectually engaged, I see them reading and interpreting quality literature, perhaps on their own, with a partner, or in small groups. They may be responding to teacher-developed open-ended response sheets or generating their own responses from a menu of options.

Grouping Practices and Independent Student Activities

This leads me to two other related and intertwined aspects of expert classroom reading instruction, effective grouping practices and worthwhile, independent student activities. Effective teachers provide a good balance between whole-class and small-group instruction (Taylor & Peterson, 2006a, 2006b, 2006c). Not surprisingly, having almost all whole-group or almost all small-group instruction has not been found to be beneficial to students' overall reading growth. Too much whole-group instruction typically leads to high levels of passive student responding. Too much small-group instruction leads to large amounts of independent or partner "seatwork" time for students. Often these seatwork activities engage students in low-level cognitive tasks, completed with apparent low levels of energy, such as completing fill-in-the-blank workbook pages; playing phonics games; copying spelling words; listening to stories on tape with no follow-up; or reading and rereading books that are too easy (Taylor & Peterson,

2006c). In contrast, students appear more motivated when I see them engaged in activities such as reading quality fiction and nonfiction that is at their instructional level, writing discussion questions and comprehension-monitoring queries on sticky notes, working with a partner to answer high-level questions about a story, or reading informational text and taking notes to write a report.

Teacher and Student Actions

Two additional aspects of classroom reading instruction for teachers to consider are their stance toward instruction and the amount of active pupil involvement in literacy learning they provide for their students. As I visit elementary classrooms, it appears that teachers often do not consciously reflect on their stance toward instruction. Effective teachers have a good balance between the use of a teacher-directed stance and a student-support stance (Connor, Morrison, & Katch, 2004; Taylor et al., 2003). They say to themselves, I need to use a teacher-directed stance here because I have information to tell to the students, or This was an especially hard story, so I will ask them questions about what they have read to monitor their comprehension. At other times they will tell themselves, I am going to be using a student-support stance right now because I need to provide coaching and feedback as students are engaged in a learning activity I have structured for them. Both stances are important. However, in general, research has found very high levels of telling and leading of recitations by teachers (e.g., almost all of the time) and very low levels of coaching (e.g., seldom) to be negatively related to students' reading growth (Taylor et al., 2003; Taylor & Peterson, 2006a, 2006c).

Teachers also need to carefully balance the amount of time that students are passively involved in their literacy learning (e.g., listening to the teacher or waiting for their turn in round-robin reading) with the amount of time that students are actively participating (e.g., reading on their own instead of listening to someone else read; writing thoughts about a story in a journal to share later in small group). Research has found that high levels of active responding are positively related to students' reading growth (Taylor & Pearson, 2004). As I visit classrooms and see relatively large numbers of students off task, it usually is because the teacher is teaching from a teacher-directed stance over an extended period of time and students are given little opportunity to actively participate in the lesson.

Time Spent on Reading

Effective teachers spend 120–135 minutes per day on reading instruction in the primary grades (Taylor et al., 2000; Taylor & Peterson, 2003). However, time spent on reading instruction alone won't make the difference that is needed to raise the bar and close the achievement gap in high poverty, diverse schools. The substantial commitment to total minutes of reading instruction in the elementary school day needs to be minutes of effective instruction that meets students' varying needs. Also, classroom teachers and resource teachers need time to plan together, and they need to use this time efficiently and effectively to coordinate the reading instruction students receive.

Alignment of Standards, Curriculum, Instruction, and Assessments

In recent years, district staff have provided leadership for schools in aligning standards, instruction, and assessment. I perceive that this is largely because of state efforts to revise standards and assessments related to reading under No Child Left Behind. At the school level, many teachers struggle with balancing the coverage of content necessary to help students reach state standards and pass required tests without losing sight of the more general goal of teaching students to be competent, motivated readers and independent learners. Teachers need to have heartfelt discussions with each other about the balance between covering the basics and teaching for lifelong learning. By focusing on good instruction and using instructional materials wisely, teachers can provide the effective reading instruction necessary for students to achieve state standards, pass required tests, and perhaps most important, become successful, thinking, independent readers and learners.

Conclusion

When teachers implement practices associated with improved reading outcomes (see those stated above), students are better readers. This requires long-term, school-based professional development in which teachers learn together about research-based practices, support each other as they implement new strategies and techniques, and reflect on their teaching to become even more effective. Many schools are engaged in schoolwide reading improvement efforts and are working hard to teach all students to read well in the elementary grades. Teachers are learning new instructional routines in workshops and are trying out newly purchased materials. Schools are hiring literacy coaches who provide support to teachers in their classrooms. Time for reading instruction may have increased and uninterrupted blocks of time for reading may have been scheduled. However, without all teachers reflecting on their practice and trying to provide the most effective, differentiated instruction possible to meet all students' needs, these efforts won't suffice. We know that when effective Tier 1 instruction is in place, the number of students who require intervention and supplemental instruction is reduced.

> **Serious efforts to improve teaching practices are important missing pieces of most schoolwide reading improvement efforts.**

From my 10 years of studying schoolwide reading improvement efforts and effective classroom reading instruction and in my many visits to schools and classrooms over these years, I believe that serious efforts to improve teaching practices are important missing pieces of most schoolwide reading improvement efforts. In short, teachers need to work together to reflect on and maximize the effectiveness of their reading instruction. Leaders need to provide the support and encouragement necessary to make this possible. Fortunately, by working together within a building, teachers can make a real difference in their students' success as readers.

REFERENCES

Adams, M.J. (1990). *Beginning to read: Thinking and learning about print.* Cambridge, MA: MIT Press.

Afflerbach, P. (2006, December). *The use of the terms "reading skill" and "reading strategy" in professional discourse.* Paper presented at the annual meeting of the National Reading Conference, Los Angeles, CA.

Au, K. (2006). *Multicultural issues and literacy achievement.* Mahwah, NJ: Erlbaum.

Baumann, J.F., & Kame'enui, E.J. (2004). *Vocabulary instruction: Research to practice.* New York: Guilford.

Beck, I.L., McKeown, M.G., & Kucan, L. (2002). *Bringing words to life: Robust vocabulary instruction.* New York: Guilford.

Blachowicz, C.L.Z., & Fisher, P.J. (2000). Vocabulary instruction. In M.L. Kamil, P. Mosenthal, P.D. Pearson, & R. Barr (Eds.), *Handbook of reading research* (Vol. 3, pp. 503–523). Mahwah, NJ: Erlbaum.

Connor, C.M., Morrison, F.J., & Katch, L.E. (2004). Beyond the reading wars: Exploring the effect of child-instruction interactions on growth in early reading. *Scientific Studies of Reading, 8*(4), 305–336.

Duffy, G.G., Roehler, L.R., Sivan, E., Rackliffe, G., Book, C., Meloth, M.S., et al. (1987). Effects of explaining the reasoning associated with using reading strategies. *Reading Research Quarterly, 22*(3), 347–368.

Ehri, L. (1991). Development of the ability to read words. In R. Barr, M.L. Kamil, P. Mosenthal, & P.D. Pearson (Eds.), *Handbook of reading research* (Vol. 2, pp. 383–417). White Plains, NY: Longman.

Garcia, G.E., Taylor, B.M., & Pearson, P.D. (2006, April). *Improving students' reading comprehension in grades 2–5.* Symposium presented at the annual meeting of the American Educational Research Association, San Francisco, CA.

Graves, M. (2007). Conceptual and empirical bases for providing struggling readers with multifaceted and long-term vocabulary instruction. In B.M. Taylor & J.E. Ysseldyke (Eds.), *Effective instruction for struggling readers, K–6.* New York: Teachers College Press.

Guthrie, J.T., Wigfield, A., Barbosa, P., Perencevich, K.C., Taboada, A., Davis, M.H., et al. (2004). Increasing reading comprehension and engagement through concept-oriented reading instruction. *Journal of Educational Psychology, 96*(3), 403–423.

Guthrie, J.T., Wigfield, A., & Von Secker, C. (2000). Effects of integrated instruction on motivation and strategy use in reading. *Journal of Educational Psychology, 92*(2), 331–341.

Knapp, M.S. (1995). *Teaching for meaning in high-poverty classrooms.* New York: Teachers College Press.

Kuhn, M.R., & Stahl, S.A. (2003). Fluency: A review of developmental and remedial practices. *Journal of Educational Psychology, 95*(1), 3–21.

Lipson, M. (2007). *Teaching reading beyond the primary grades.* New York: Scholastic.

Nagy, W.E., & Scott, J.A. (2000). Vocabulary processes. In M.L. Kamil, P. Mosenthal, P.D. Pearson, & R. Barr (Eds.), *Handbook of reading research* (Vol. 3, pp. 269–284). Mahwah, NJ: Erlbaum.

National Institute of Child Health and Human Development. (2000). *Report of the National Reading Panel. Teaching students to read: An evidence-based assessment of the scientific research literature on reading and its implications for reading instruction* (NIH Publication No. 00-4769). Washington, DC: U.S. Government Printing Office.

Paris, S. (2005). Reinterpreting the development of reading skills. *Reading Research Quarterly, 40*(2), 184–202.

Pressley, M. (2006). *Reading instruction that works: The case for balanced teaching* (3rd ed.). New York: Guilford.

Pressley, M., Dolezal, S.E., Raphael, L.M., Mohan, L., Roehrig, A.D., & Bogner, K. (2003). *Motivating primary-grade students.* New York: Guilford.

Snow, C.E., Burns, M.S., & Griffin, P. (Eds.). (1998). *Preventing reading difficulties in young students.* Washington, DC: National Academy Press.

Stahl, S.A. (2001). Teaching phonics and phonemic awareness. In S.B. Neuman & D. Dickenson (Eds.), *Handbook of early literacy research* (pp. 333–347). New York: Guilford.

Stahl, S.A. (2004). What do we know about fluency? Findings of the National Reading Panel. In P. McCardle & V. Chhabra (Eds.), *The voice of evidence in reading research* (pp. 187–212). Baltimore: Paul Brookes.

Taylor, B.M., & Pearson, P.D. (2004). Research on learning to read—at school, at home, and in the community. *The Elementary School Journal, 105*(2), 167–181.

Taylor, B.M., Pearson, P.D., Clark, K., & Walpole, S. (2000). Effective schools and accomplished teachers: Lessons about primary-grade reading instruction in low-income schools. *The Elementary School Journal, 101*(2), 121–165.

Taylor, B.M., Pearson, P.D., Peterson, D.S., & Rodriguez, M.C. (2003). Reading growth in high-poverty classrooms: The influence of teacher practices that encourage cognitive engagement in literacy learning. *The Elementary School Journal, 104*(1), 3–28.

Taylor, B.M., Pearson, P.D., Peterson, D.S., & Rodriguez, M.C. (2005). The CIERA School Change Framework: An evidence-based approach to professional development and school reading improvement. *Reading Research Quarterly, 40*(1), 40–69.

Taylor, B.M., & Peterson, D.S. (2003). *Year 1 report of the Minnesota REA School Change project.* St. Paul: University of Minnesota, Minnesota Center for Reading Research.

Taylor, B.M., & Peterson, D.S. (2006a). *The impact of the School Change Framework in twenty-three Minnesota REA schools.* St. Paul: University of Minnesota, Minnesota Center for Reading Research.

Taylor, B.M., & Peterson, D.S. (2006b). *Year 3 report of the Minnesota Reading First Cohort 1 School Change project.* St. Paul: University of Minnesota, Minnesota Center for Reading Research.

Taylor, B.M., & Peterson, D.S. (2006c). *Year 1 report of the Minnesota Reading First Cohort 2 School Change project.* St. Paul: University of Minnesota, Minnesota Center for Reading Research.

Taylor, B.M., & Peterson, D.S. (2007). *Year 2 report of the Minnesota Reading First Cohort 2 School Change project.* St. Paul: University of Minnesota, Minnesota Center for Reading Research.

The Role of Assessment Within the RTI Framework

Lynn S. Fuchs and Douglas Fuchs

Within an RTI approach, assessment plays an integral role. As previously mentioned, most RTI models are framed within a multi-tier prevention system. General education constitutes primary prevention (see Chapter 1 in this book on primary intervention). Students who fail to respond to this general, or "universal," core program enter the RTI process with secondary prevention. In most research studies, this involves one or more rounds of research-based small-group tutoring. Students who respond poorly to this more intensive form of secondary prevention are thought to demonstrate "unexpected failure" and become candidates for tertiary intervention (see Chapter 3, this volume, on secondary intervention). Between secondary and tertiary prevention levels, students undergo an abbreviated evaluation, designed to answer questions arising during the first two levels of prevention and to eliminate other forms of disability (if they are suspected) as a cause for unresponsiveness. Tertiary prevention is the most intensive form of instruction, involving individualized programming and progress monitoring (see Chapter 4 in this book on tertiary intervention). When adequate performance is achieved, students exit to return to secondary or primary prevention.

Response to Intervention: A Framework for Reading Educators edited by Douglas Fuchs, Lynn S. Fuchs, and Sharon Vaughn. Copyright 2008 by the International Reading Association.

In this chapter, we focus on formal classroom assessment—when a teacher administers objective tests to measure students' abilities, skills, and strategies. Four types of assessment are available to guide teachers as they design their instruction: screening, progress monitoring, diagnosis, and outcome evaluation. In this chapter, we limit our attention to screening and progress monitoring, the most essential assessment functions within RTI, and we limit our discussion to reading (for information on mathematics, see Fuchs & Fuchs, 2008). For each type of assessment, we explain its purpose and describe a tool designed to fulfill that function in the area of reading. Finally, we explain how these types of assessment connect to instruction within a multi-tier prevention system.

Screening

With screening, a large number of students are measured at one point in time (usually at the beginning of the school year), on a brief test. The purpose is to select the subset of students who, without special attention, are in danger of reading failure. The goal of screening is to identify students who are at risk of reading failure so that prevention services can be provided to these students as quickly as possible. The hope is that early prevention will improve the long-term outcomes of these students, avoiding the chronic and severe difficulties that students with learning disabilities face throughout school and in their adult lives.

Currently, the most commonly used screening tool in the United States is the Dynamic Indicators of Basic Early Literacy Skills, or DIBELS. Designed for use at kindergarten through third grade levels (more recent extensions span through sixth grade), DIBELS incorporates a system of measures. Each measure comes with two cut scores to designate three categories of students. Those below the lowest cut score are "at risk" for failure; for these students "substantial intervention" is recommended. Students who are below a second cut score are deemed as having "some risk" for reading failure; for these students "additional intervention" is recommended. Students above this second cut score are considered to be at "low risk" for reading failure; they are deemed to be "at grade level" in reading so that no adjustment in reading program is warranted. Different cut scores are provided depending on whether screening occurs at the beginning of the school year or at the middle of the school year. Here we focus exclusively on screening at the beginning of kindergarten and first grade, which is most typically when schools screen to identify students whose prospects for reading development are poor.

At the kindergarten level, DIBELS relies on three measures. With letter naming fluency, the student is presented with a printed page containing upper- and lowercase letters and is asked to name as many letters as possible in one minute. The score is the number of letters named correctly. Alternate pages display the letters in different, random orders. Another DIBELS measure at the kindergarten level is initial sound fluency. The student says the word or selects the picture of a word that begins with a target sound from an array of four pictures. For example, the examiner says, "This is a sink, cat, gloves, and a hat. Which picture begins with /s/?" After asking the question, the examiner starts the stopwatch and stops it as soon as the student says a word or picks a picture. Each alternate page of the initial sound fluency test contains nine items for which the student points to or says the name of the picture. For every fourth item, however, the student produces the onset sound for the target word (e.g., says, /s/). The score is calculated by dividing the total time taken to respond to all items by the number of correct responses and flipping this quotient to indicate the number of initial sounds correct per minute. A third and more difficult measure is phoneme segmentation fluency, in which the examiner says words for one minute; after each word, the student produces the word in segmented sounds. The score is the number of correct phonemes across the words. DIBELS suggests that schools test students on two DIBELS measures at the beginning of kindergarten: letter naming fluency and initial sound fluency. Using multiple measures together, each with its own cut score, may improve the detection of students who are at risk of developing long-term, serious reading problems. It also may reduce the number of students who are falsely identified as at risk of difficulty.

At the first-grade level, DIBELS suggests the combined use of three screening measures at the beginning of the year: (1) letter naming fluency (see previous description), (2) phoneme segmentation fluency (again, see previous description), and (3) nonsense-word fluency. With nonsense-word fluency, the student is presented with a page with randomly ordered vowel–consonant and consonant–vowel–consonant pseudowords and asked to respond in one of two ways: to say the individual letter sounds in each pseudoword or to decode the pseudoword. The student has one minute to produce as many sounds as possible; when a word is decoded, credit is awarded for each correct sound produced in the decoding. Alternate pages present various pseudowords randomly sampled from a large pool of pseudowords. As with all assessments at the kindergarten level, determining risk status on one or more of the three measures at the beginning of first grade still produces errors in identifying students who will fare well versus those who will fare poorly. Too many students are identified as at risk, because some go on to develop adequate reading skill without special intervention. These errors are costly for schools because the schools tutor these students even though they do not require it. In addition, too many students who will eventually develop serious reading problems are missed. These are serious errors because they compromise the very purpose of screening.

As illustrated with DIBELS at kindergarten and at first grade, it may be difficult for a one-time screening test, regardless of what measure or combination of measures is used, to provide schools with a highly precise specification of which students are and are not at risk. On the basis of our research (Compton, Fuchs, Fuchs, & Bryant, 2006), then, we have combined screening with progress monitoring. That is, we screen all students at the beginning of the school year. We recommend using a screening cut score that identifies a relatively large pool of students: those below the 50th percentile. These students, however, are "suspected" to be at risk, rather than deemed to be at risk, and schools do not immediately provide any additional services to these students. The idea is to cast a wide net so that no student who might develop severe reading problems is missed. Then, these students (who are suspected to be at risk) complete brief, weekly progress monitoring assessments (as discussed in the next section) for six to eight weeks. The progress monitoring scores are used to determine which students suspected to be at risk are gradually improving over these six to eight weeks. Demonstration of progress disconfirms the suspicion of risk. If, however, students fail to demonstrate progress over these six to eight weeks, the suspected risk is confirmed and a secondary tutoring intervention is then instituted to improve the at-risk students' progress.

> It may be difficult for a one-time screening test to provide schools with a highly precise specification of which students are and are not at risk.

Progress Monitoring

With progress monitoring, students are assessed frequently (i.e., at least monthly). Their scores are graphed against time, and a line of best fit is drawn through the graphed points. For this line of best fit, a slope (i.e., the weekly rate of increase) is calculated to quantify the rate of learning. Teachers can use the progress monitoring slope, along with the student's current score, for two purposes: (1) to determine whether a student is responding adequately to the instructional program and (2) to inductively design individualized instructional plans for students who are unresponsive to a validated or research-based instructional program. Two major forms of progress monitoring are mastery measurement and general outcome measurement (see Fuchs & Deno, 1991).

Mastery Measurement

With mastery measurement, teachers assess mastery of a sequence of skills. Designing a mastery measurement progress monitoring system requires two major tasks. The first requires determining the hierarchy of skills for instruction. For example, with first-grade reading, one might specify the following sequence of skills: letter–sound correspondence, decoding phonemically regular consonant–vowel–consonant words, decoding phonemically regular consonant–vowel–consonant–final *e* words, automatically recognizing the 100 most frequent Dolch words, decoding phonemically regular *r*-controlled words, and so on. The second major task in designing a mastery measurement progress monitoring system is to design a criterion-referenced test for each skill in the instructional hierarchy. For example, for letter–sound correspondence, the criterion-referenced test might involve

© 2008 JupiterImages Corporation

presenting students with a shuffled deck of letters, one letter at a time for one minute. The student responds by saying the sounds associated with the letters; the score is the number of correct sounds. The criterion for mastery might be 26 letter sounds in one minute on two consecutive tests. The test might be administered once weekly and when the student achieves the mastery criterion, the instruction and testing simultaneously shift to the next skill in the hierarchy. This next skill is decoding phonemically regular consonant–vowel–consonant words, for which a criterion-referenced test is also designed. Most classroom-based reading assessments fall into the category of mastery measurement.

Most basal reading assessments provide unit tests to assess mastery of skills addressed in each unit. Nevertheless, research (e.g., Tindal et al., 1985) indicates that few classroom teachers adhere to mastery rules, based on those tests, for advancing students to new instructional content. In addition, mastery measurement systems are beset by some technical problems (e.g., Tindal et al., 1985). For example, it is possible that achievement as demonstrated on the mastery measurement system (i.e., mastery of many skills across a school year) fails to relate well to performance at the end of the year on high-stakes tests. Poor correspondence, with some students who have mastered many skills performing surprisingly poorly on the high-stakes end-of-year testing, can occur because of poor retention of previously mastered skills. For example, a student might master consonant–vowel–consonant words, but when instruction and testing simultaneously shift to the next skill in the hierarchy, the student's accuracy in decoding consonant–vowel–consonant words deteriorates. Another source of poor correspondence between number of skills mastered and final performance on the high-stakes test is mastery measurement's reliance on single-skill testing framework. Some students can perform a skill competently only because they know that every item on the test represents an example of the target skill. For example, some students decode consonant–vowel–consonant words accurately when all the words on the test represent that pattern; students know to incorporate the short vowel for every word on the test. Some subset of these students cannot, however, decode consonant–vowel–consonant words when they are presented in mixed-skill fashion along with words of a variety of phonetic categories. In contrast to mastery measurement, high-stakes tests do not rely on single-skill measurement. Hence the potential exists for a lack of correspondence between performance on mastery measurement's single-skill testing framework versus performance on high-stakes tests' sampling across many skills.

General Outcome Measurement

For these and other reasons, over the past 30 years an alternative form of progress monitoring has been developed and has gained popularity. This alternative form of progress monitoring is known as general outcome measurement. General outcome measurement simultaneously assesses performance across the many skills represented in the annual curriculum. Research indicates that general outcome progress monitoring represents a technically superior framework for progress monitoring, relating better to end-of-year high-stakes test performance.

General outcome measurement differs from most forms of classroom assessment in three ways. First, general outcome measurement is standardized so that the behaviors to be measured and the procedures for measuring those behaviors are prescribed. This ensures that the assessment scores are accurate and meaningful. Second, the focus of general outcome measurement is long term so that testing methods and content remain constant. That is, each weekly test is of equivalent difficulty and spans the entire school year. The primary reason for long-term consistency is so that teachers can compare scores from September to scores collected at any other time of year to determine whether the student has improved. Third, general outcome measurement is fluency based so that students have a fixed amount of time to respond to the test. Therefore, improvement reflects an individual's capacity to perform critical behaviors with accuracy and with ease.

Curriculum-based measurement (CBM) is the form of general outcome progress monitoring for which most of the research has been conducted (see, for example, Fuchs & Fuchs, 1998). CBM can take one of two forms. It can systematically sample the curriculum or can rely on a single behavior that functions as an overall indicator of competence in an academic area. In reading, most CBM systems rely on the overall indicator approach.

At kindergarten, the major alternatives for CBM reading measures are phoneme segmentation fluency, rapid letter naming, and letter sound fluency. (We note that at kindergarten and the other grades, progress monitoring measures mirror the screening measures already discussed because the screening measures were derived from the progress monitoring literature.) With phoneme segmentation fluency, the examiner says a word; the student says its constituent sounds. The examiner provides as many stimuli within one minute as the rate of the student's response permits. With rapid letter naming, the examiner presents a page of lower- and uppercase letters randomly ordered; the student says as many letter names as he or she can in one minute. With letter sound fluency, the examiner also presents a page with lower- and uppercase letters randomly ordered; this time, however, the student says sounds for one minute. Compared with phoneme segmentation fluency, rapid letter naming and letter sound fluency are easier for practitioners to learn to administer, and reliability tends to be stronger. On the other hand, compared with rapid letter naming, phoneme segmentation fluency and letter sound fluency are better targets for instruction because they relate more transparently to what students need to learn to read. For this reason, it is possible that phoneme segmentation fluency and letter sound fluency will guide the kindergarten teacher's instructional behavior more effectively.

At first grade, two CBM reading measures have been studied. One approach, typified in DIBELS, involves combining nonsense-word fluency and passage reading fluency: Students begin the year on nonsense-word fluency and move to the more difficult performance indicator, passage reading fluency, in January. With nonsense-word fluency (Fuchs, Fuchs, & Compton, 2004), students are presented with a page of consonant-vowel-consonant (with some vowel-consonant) pseudowords and have one minute to decode as many as they can. With passage reading fluency, students are presented with grade-level text (each alternate page is a passage of roughly equivalent difficulty), and students read aloud for one minute. Alternatively, schools use a constant measure across all of first grade: word identification fluency, where students are presented with a page showing 50 high-frequency words (each alternate page samples words from a list of 100 words and presents the 50 in random order); students read as many words as possible in one minute. The advantage of nonsense-word fluency is that it maps onto beginning decoding instruction (at least consonant–vowel–consonant patterns), potentially providing teachers with input for instructional planning. The disadvantage of the nonsense-word fluency/passage reading fluency combination is that getting a good picture of development over the course of first grade is problematic. That is, teachers cannot compare scores collected in the first half of the year with scores collected after passage reading fluency begins. By contrast, word identification fluency can be used with strong reliability, validity, and instructional usefulness across the entire first-grade year. This also makes it possible to get a good picture of a student's reading development across the entire time frame.

At the second and third grade levels, the CBM passage reading fluency measure (Fuchs, Fuchs, Hosp, & Jenkins, 2001) provides the strongest source of information on reading development. Each week, one test is administered, with the student reading aloud from a different but equivalent passage for one minute; the examiner counts the number of words read correctly within the one-minute time frame. The reliability, validity, and instructional utility of this simple measure have been demonstrated repeatedly. Some teachers can think of students whose comprehension is weak despite good fluency. This, however, is rare. In fact, these cases are so unusual that they are highly memorable. In the vast majority of cases, students who have strong fluency are the same students who also demonstrate good comprehension.

Some research indicates that the validity of the CBM passage reading fluency task begins to decrease beginning at fourth or fifth grade (see Espin, 2006). Beginning at this level, teachers should consider using a different measure that more directly taps comprehension. One alternative for the higher grades is CBM maze fluency. With maze fluency, the student is presented with a passage from which every seventh word has been deleted and replaced with three possible replacements, only one of which is semantically tenable. The student has two or three minutes to read and replace blanks, and the score is the number of correct replacements (with three consecutive errors used as a ceiling). Some research indicates that maze fluency demonstrates strong reliability and validity and models reading development beginning at fourth grade and continuing through eighth grade.

These CBM strategies for characterizing reading growth have been shown to be more sensitive for detecting student improvement than other classroom reading tests. In addition, CBM has been shown to reveal student improvement regardless of whether teachers rely on explicit instruction or whole language. Also, with CBM, teachers incorporate a wide range of instructional methods including, for example, decoding instruction, repeated readings, vocabulary instruction, story grammar exercises, and semantic mapping activities. So CBM is not tied to any particular instructional approach. This permits teachers to experiment with instructional adaptations or major program revisions in an attempt to effect progress for students for whom the standard reading program proves ineffective. Research shows that when teachers use CBM progress monitoring to help them tailor their instruction to match students' instructional needs, teachers plan better instructional programs and they effect better achievement among students. (For a synthesis of research on CBM, see Fuchs & Fuchs, 1998.)

Teachers can use CBM to help shape effective programs at the class level or for an individual student for whom the standard curriculum proves ineffective. At the class level, CBM progress monitoring data can be reported to teachers in ways that help them design better reading programs. For example, Figure 2.1 is a CBM Class Summary for a second-grade class (all student names are pseudonyms). The top of the first page shows a class graph: The lowest data path indicates the trajectory of improvement for the students in the lowest quartile of that teacher's class; the middle data path indicates the trajectory of improvement for the students in the middle two quartiles of that teacher's class; and the highest data path indicates the trajectory of improvement for the students in the highest quartile of that teacher's class lists students. Below the class graph, the summary identifies "Students to Watch" (i.e., students who are below the 25th percentile of that teacher's class) and "Most Improved" (i.e., students who have demonstrated the greatest improvement during the previous month).

Page 3 of the CBM Class Summary lists students ranked from highest to lowest performing in terms of their most recent CBM scores. These CBM scores are shown along with each student's present weekly CBM slope of improvement. For example, a teacher can see that Ethan Hunter has a high CBM score with a good rate of weekly improvement; Shane Moss has a relatively low CBM score but is showing a good rate of weekly improvement; and Gregory

FIGURE 2.1

CBM Class Summary

Class Summary
Teacher: Hoover
Report through 12/17

Students to Watch

Shane Moss
Yolanda Navarro
Maria Argueta
Teresa Rodriguez
Gregory Brown

Most Improved

Teresa Rodriguez
Tanasha Storey
Nicholas Norton
Ethan Hunter
Ashley Anderson

Comprehension Activities

Alex Gray	Ethan Hunter
Alicia Scott	Janice Andrews
Ashley Anderson	Nathaniel Dunbar
David Jackson	Paul Minton
Donald Harrison	Victor Sandoval

Fluency Practice

Mica Netter
Nicholas Norton
Terrance Reeves

Phonics Instruction

MAT/LAST	TIME	CAR	BEAT	HAPPY	PUBLIC	RUNNING
Gregory Brown	Gregory Brown	Yolanda Navarro	Shane Moss		Benjamine Everson	
Maria Argueta	Maria Argueta				Tanasha Storey	
Teresa Rodriguez	Shane Moss					
William Douglas	Teresa Rodriguez					
	William Douglas					
	Yolanda Navarro					

(continued)

FIGURE 2.1 (continued)

CBM Class Summary

Class Skills Profile
Teacher: Hoover
Report through 12/17

Name	Comprehension	Fluency	MAT/LAST	TIME	CAR	BEAT	HAPPY	PUBLIC	RUNNING
Alex Gray	C								
Alicia Scott	C								
Ashley Anderson	C								
Benjamine Everson			■	■	■	■	■	⊞	■
David Jackson	C								
Donald Harrison	C								
Ethan Hunter	C								
Gregory Brown			⊞	III	III	III	III	III	III
Janice Andrews	C								
Maria Argueta			III	III	III	III	⊞	III	⊞
Mica Netter		F							
Nathaniel Dunbar	C								
Nicholas Norton		F							
Paul Minton	C								
Shane Moss			■	⊞	■	⊞	■	■	■
Tanasha Storey			■	■	■	■	■	⊞	■
Teresa Rodriguez			III	III	III	III	III	III	III
Terrance Reeves		F							
Victor Sandoval	C								
William Douglas			⊞	III	⊞	⊞	■	⊞	■
Yolanda Navarro			■	III	⊞	⊞	III	III	III

III Cold. Missing most of these words.

⊞ Warm. Getting some of these words right.

■ Hot. Getting most of these words right.

MAT/LAST: closed syllable, short vowel (e.g., bed, top, hit, cat, bump, mast, damp)
TIME: final e, long vowel (e.g., cake, poke, same, woke, mine, rose, gate)
CAR: vowel r-controlled (e.g., fur, nor, per, sir, her, tar)
BEAT: two vowels together (e.g., soap, maid, lean, loaf, paid, meal)
HAPPY: divide between two like consonants (e.g., lesson, bubble, battle, giggle)
PUBLIC: divide between unlike consonants (e.g., elbow, walrus, doctor, victim, admit)
RUNNING: dividing between double consonant with suffix (e.g., batter, sipped, hitting, tanned, bitten)

(continued)

FIGURE 2.1 (continued)

CBM Class Summary

Class Scores
Teacher: Hoover
Report through 12/17

Name	Score	Growth
**** Already on grade level		
Ethan Hunter	132	+4.86
Victor Sandoval	130	+2.36
Alicia Scott	121	+4.51
Alex Gray	117	+3.92
Nathaniel Dunbar	106	+0.90
David Jackson	104	+1.56
Paul Minton	95	+1.59
Ashley Anderson	95	+2.38
Janice Andrews	93	+0.56
Donald Harrison	85	+2.44
Mica Netter	81	+0.89
Nicholas Norton	80	+3.44
**** On track for completing year on grade level		
Terrance Reeves	68	+2.57
Benjamine Everson	66	+1.23
Tanasha Storey	60	+3.50
**** At risk for completing grade below grade level		
William Douglas	44	+1.50
Shane Moss	41	+2.12
Yolanda Navarro	30	+1.52
Maria Argueta	29	+0.38
Teresa Rodriguez	24	+2.36
Gregory Brown	8	+0.88

(continued)

CBM Class Summary

Class Statistics
Teacher: Hoover
Report through 5/27

Score		Slope	
Average score	84.5	Average slope	+1.84
Standard deviation	37.0	Standard deviation	1.11
Discrepancy criterion	47.5	Discrepancy criterion	+0.73

Students identified with dual discrepancy criterion

	Score	Slope
Gregory Brown	10.5	+0.30

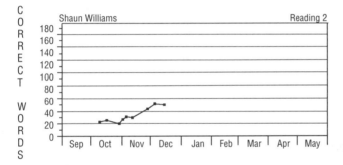

MAT/LAST
TIME
CAR
BEAT
HAPPY
PUBLIC
RUNNING

▥ Cold. Missing most of these words.

▦ Warm. Getting some of these words right.

■ Hot. Getting most of these words right.

MAT/LAST: closed syllable, short vowel (e.g., bed, top, hit, cat, bump, mast, damp)

TIME: final e, long vowel (e.g., cake, poke, same, woke, mine, rose, gate)

CAR: vowel r-controlled (e.g., fur, nor, per, sir, her, tar)

BEAT: two vowels together (e.g., soap, maid, lean, loaf, paid, meal)

HAPPY: divide between two like consonants (e.g., lesson, bubble, battle, giggle)

PUBLIC: divide between unlike consonants (e.g., elbow, walrus, doctor, victim, admit)

RUNNING: dividing between double consonant with suffix (e.g., batter, sipped, hitting, tanned, bitten)

Brown, by contrast, has a very low CBM score and an inadequate rate of improvement. Students in the class are grouped in terms of those whose current performance already meets end-of-grade CBM expectations; those who have not yet achieved the end-of-year benchmark but are on track for goal attainment; and students who are at risk of completing the year below the end-of-year benchmark.

On page 4, class statistics are provided that potentially inform decisions about which students require a level of intervention that exceeds what is ordinarily provided within general education. Using terminology borrowed from multi-tier prevention systems, this would mean secondary (e.g., small-group tutoring using a validated tutoring protocol) or tertiary intervention (e.g., instruction that is individually tailored and more intensive, in terms of student–teacher ratio and time). On page 4, the mean CBM score for the class is shown, along with the standard deviation on that mean and a discrepancy CBM score (average score minus 1 standard deviation) for signaling an inadequate performance level relative to classmates. The same information is shown for slope (i.e., weekly rate of improvement). Then, students meeting a "dual discrepancy criterion" (i.e., 1+ standard deviation below the class mean on performance level and slope) are listed so that the teacher can consider referral to secondary intervention for these students who are at high risk for reading failure. In Mrs. Hoover's class, Gregory Brown meets the dual discrepancy criterion. If secondary intervention fails to move the student above the dual discrepancy criterion, then tertiary intervention would be considered. In this way, for a student identified by the dual discrepancy criterion as not benefiting from the general education core reading program (which benefits the vast majority of students), classroom modifications to the reading program can be instituted (keeping the student within general education, or Tier 1 of a multi-tier prevention system). If classroom modifications fail to substantially improve the student's CBM score and slope of improvement, then the student might receive additional intervention. For example, small-group tutoring might be used in Tier 2 of the multi-tier prevention system.

When additional intervention such as small-group tutoring fails to enhance performance, schools need to consider the possibility that the student requires an individually tailored program to meet the student's special needs. This typically occurs at third tier within the multi-tier prevention system and under the auspices of special education. At Tier 3, CBM informs instructional planning using the graphed performance indicator. If a student's growth trajectory is judged to be adequate, the teacher increases the student's goal for year-end performance; if judged inadequate, the teacher revises the instructional program. Research shows that with these CBM decision rules, teachers design more varied instructional programs that are more responsive to individual needs, that incorporate more ambitious student goals, and that result in stronger end-of-year scores on commercial, standardized reading tests.

Tightening the Link Between Assessment and Instruction: Using an RTI Multi-Tier Prevention System

As discussed at the beginning of this chapter, RTI has been conceptualized within a multi-tier prevention system that typically incorporates three tiers, with each tier providing increasingly more intensive instruction. General education is the first tier. The second tier is typically accomplished with a standard, validated, small-group tutoring protocol. When this tutoring proves unsuccessful for a given student, then a third tier of intervention is implemented. This third tier is typically individualized to meet the students' special learning needs.

Why is a multi-tier prevention system important? The answer is that no instructional method, even instructional procedures that have been validated using stringent experimental studies, works for all students. For this reason, as schools implement validated interventions, even those that have been scientifically validated, the effects of those interventions on each student's reading performance must be assessed. This is why assessment is an essential component of RTI, of a multi-tier prevention system, of Reading First, and of any school's effort to enhance the effectiveness of its reading program. When systematic assessment is integrated in a meaningful way with the life of a reading instructional program, students who do not respond adequately to the classroom program can be identified promptly for a second tier of more intensive intervention. For students who fail to respond to this second level of programming, a third tier of instruction with greater individualization is implemented, and response continues to be assessed. This iterative process, with which interventions of increasing intensity and individualization are conducted and their effects are continuously assessed, describes a multi-tiered prevention system. Within a multi-tiered prevention system, therefore, assessment plays three important roles:

> As schools implement validated interventions, even those that have been scientifically validated, the effects of those interventions on each student's reading performance must be assessed.

1. Identifying students who should be targeted for attention
2. Quantifying responsiveness to intervention among those targeted for attention
3. Tailoring individualized instructional programs for the most unresponsive subset of students

Within this scheme, the first assessment function is identifying a subset of the school population that is suspected to be at risk for poor reading outcomes. These students become the focus of the multi-tier prevention system. This first function is referred to as screening. With screening, a brief measure is administered to all students in a school or within targeted grade levels (usually the primary grades) in a school. A screening cut score is applied, which specifies what screening score is associated with inadequate performance on a valued outcome measure, such as a high-stakes

test, at a later time. All students scoring below this cut score are designated as at risk for poor outcome. This screening, which relies on a one-time test administration, is often referred to as benchmark assessment. It is not a form of progress monitoring, which requires more frequent (typically, at least monthly) assessment. As already noted, benchmark assessment for the purpose of screening carries a significant danger of identifying students for tutoring when, in fact, those students would go on to develop strong academic skills without tutoring. It can also overlook students who in fact require that tutoring.

As already described, because benchmark screening typically makes too many errors of these types (especially at kindergarten and first grade), we suggest that one-time screening assessment constitute only the first step in the process of designating risk status. That is, we recommend that students who are first *suspected* to be at risk on the basis of benchmark screening be followed with six to eight weeks of progress monitoring while Tier 1 general education is implemented. The purpose of this short-term progress monitoring is to gauge response to general education and thereby confirm that the suspected risk, on the basis of benchmark screening, probably constitutes actual risk. Such short-term progress monitoring has been shown to increase the precision of designating who requires a Tier 2 intervention and therefore avoids wasting costly Tier 2 services on students whose academic skills would develop nicely without that special intervention. Of course, best practice means using progress monitoring and diagnostic assessment even within Tier 1 toward the goal of differentiating instruction, as illustrated in Figure 2.1 on pages 39–42.

Within a multi-tier prevention system, a second purpose for progress monitoring occurs at Tier 2 where tutoring is based on standard treatment protocols. With a standard treatment protocol, a validated or research-based approach to tutoring is implemented in small groups. The assumption is that a vast majority of students should respond well to the validated or research-based small-group tutoring. If a child responds poorly to tutoring that benefits most students, then the responsiveness-to-instruction assessment process eliminates instructional quality as a viable explanation for poor academic growth and instead provides evidence of a disability. The purpose of progress monitoring at Tier 2 is to quantify student progress over the course of tutoring. That is, to determine which students do and which students do not respond to validated small-group tutoring. The students who fare well (i.e., whose progress monitoring slopes of improvement indicate adequate progress) are returned to Tier 1. There, progress monitoring is continued to assess whether the Tier 2 tutoring "inoculated" the student against further learning difficulties or whether the student instead requires another round of Tier 2 tutoring.

By contrast, students whose CBM slopes of improvement in Tier 2 tutoring are inadequate, indicating poor progress to the validated tutoring protocol, then enter tertiary, or Tier 3, intervention. This is typically conducted with special education resources and personnel. At the Tier 3 level, instruction differs from Tier 2 because it is more intensive (usually involving longer sessions and conducted in smaller groups, if not one-to-one) and individualized (rather than relying on a validated treatment protocol). At Tier 3, progress monitoring and diagnostic assessment are therefore essential for two purposes: (1) to inductively formulate the individualized instructional program that is optimal for an individual student (i.e., with progress monitoring and diagnostic assessment) and (2) to determine (this time with progress monitoring assessment, not diagnostic assessment) when the student's response to Tier 3 instruction is adequate to warrant a return to Tier 1 primary prevention (general education, with or without accommodations or modifications) or to Tier 2 small-group tutoring (using a standard treatment protocol). With return to Tier 1 or Tier 2, progress monitoring continues so that secondary or tertiary intervention can be reinitiated as needed.

Summary

In these ways, RTI, as contextualized within a multi-tier prevention system, is a useful framework by which schools can address the needs of most students for whom they are accountable. One important advantage of RTI, by which schools can improve their efforts at improving student outcome, is creating a tighter link between assessment and instruction. As illustrated in this chapter, assessment, in the form of screening and progress monitoring, is a critical component of any successful RTI multi-tier prevention system.

AUTHOR NOTE

This research was supported in part by Grant #H324C000022 from the U.S. Department of Education, Office of Special Education Programs, and Core Grant #HD15052 from the National Institute of Child Health and Human Development to Vanderbilt University. Statements in this chapter do not reflect the position or policy of any of these organizations.

REFERENCES

Compton, D.L., Fuchs, D., Fuchs, L.S., & Bryant, J.D. (2006). Selecting at-risk readers in first grade for early intervention: A two-year longitudinal study of decision rules and procedures. *Journal of Educational Psychology, 98*(4), 394–409.

Espin, C. (2006, February). *The technical features of reading measures.* Paper presented at the annual meeting of the Pacific Coast Research Conference, San Diego, CA.

Fuchs, L.S., & Deno, S.L. (1991). Paradigmatic distinctions between instructionally relevant measurement models. *Exceptional Children, 57*(6), 488–499.

Fuchs, L.S., & Fuchs, D. (1998). Treatment validity: A unifying concept for reconceptualizing the identification of learning disabilities. *Learning Disabilities Research & Practice, 13*(4), 204–219.

Fuchs, L.S., & Fuchs, D. (2008). Progress monitoring within a multi-tiered prevention system: Best practices. In J. Grimes & A. Thomas (Eds.), *Best practices in school psychology* (Vol. 5, pp. 2147–2164). Bethesda, MD: National Association of School Psychologists.

Fuchs, L.S., Fuchs, D., & Compton, D.L. (2004). Monitoring early reading development in first grade: Word identification fluency versus nonsense word fluency. *Exceptional Children, 71*(7), 7–21.

Fuchs, L.S., Fuchs, D., Hosp, M.K., & Jenkins, J.R. (2001). Oral reading fluency as an indicator of reading competence: A theoretical, empirical, and historical analysis. *Scientific Studies of Reading, 5*(3), 239–256.

Tindal, G.A., Fuchs, L.S., Fuchs, D., Shinn, M.R., Deno, S.L., & Germann, G. (1985). Empirical validation of criterion-referenced tests. *Journal of Educational Research, 78*(4), 203–209.

Tier 2: The Role of Intervention

Sharon Vaughn and Carolyn A. Denton

This chapter provides an overview of secondary prevention within a Response to Intervention (RTI) framework. Many of the practices associated with effective secondary prevention are very familiar to educators, and it is likely you are currently implementing these practices in some ways. The purpose of this chapter is to provide an integrated view of the critical elements of secondary prevention so that you can determine which of the elements you need to further develop in your educational setting. The chapter addresses the following questions: Within an RTI approach, what is secondary prevention? What are some of the key considerations when implementing a secondary intervention? How might secondary interventions be implemented in schools?

What Is Secondary Prevention?

Perhaps the best way to think of secondary prevention is that it is designed to meet the needs of at-risk readers who have not made adequate progress through primary (Tier 1) instruction. Fundamentally, primary prevention (discussed in Chapter 1) provides every student with the opportunity to access the most effective reading instruction possible. As educators, we know that for most

Response to Intervention: A Framework for Reading Educators edited by Douglas Fuchs, Lynn S. Fuchs, and Sharon Vaughn. Copyright 2008 by the International Reading Association.

students, well-developed and implemented reading curricula delivered by knowledgeable teachers will provide the adequate instruction they require to progress. However, for some students even effective primary instruction (Tier 1) is not sufficient. They require occasional and perhaps relatively short-term additional instruction or curriculum adaptations to meet their needs.

Although there are myriad ways to consider secondary intervention, typically either problem-solving or standard protocol approaches (or a combination of the two) are used to identify and provide interventions for students who require secondary prevention (Batsche et al., 2005). In a problem-solving approach to secondary prevention, educators identify the student's problem behaviorally, formulate an academic goal, and then implement an intervention and administer repeated curriculum-based measures to monitor progress toward the goal and the effectiveness of the intervention. For example, if a student's performance level and rate of growth on an oral reading fluency progress monitoring measure are both significantly below the average of the student's peers, a teacher may collaborate with a problem-solving team or a reading coach to (a) define the problem systematically, (b) establish a goal for student performance, and (c) create an individualized intervention plan to address the problem. The plan is usually implemented by the classroom teacher with the support of a reading coach or other specialist, and the student's progress is monitored. After a period of time, the effectiveness of the intervention plan is evaluated to determine whether to continue, change, or discontinue the plan (Hasbrouck & Denton, 2005). Interventions may consist of a variety of components, including adaptations of the instructional objectives, activities, delivery, or materials. For example, teachers may modify grouping practices and provide more explicit instruction with extended opportunities to practice. Teachers may also provide supplemental small-group intervention to the target student within the regular classroom setting. Problem-solving plans may sometimes address classroom management or behavioral concerns that impede the student's reading growth. Intervention plans may also specify that a reading specialist or other interventionist provide supplemental support to the student.

In a standard protocol approach to secondary prevention in reading, students at risk for serious reading difficulties are identified on the basis of their performance on assessments of reading or reading-related skills and academic goals relate to expected performance benchmarks or standards. Students are provided with research-supported interventions, and progress monitoring assessment is used to inform decisions about the need for continued secondary intervention or for more intensive interventions. In this model, students identified through systematic, schoolwide screening or benchmark assessments as being at risk for reading difficulties would receive instructional intervention employed to supplement, enhance, and support Tier 1 classroom instruction. The classroom teacher, a specialized reading teacher, or other trained personnel designated by the school typically provides intervention in homogeneous groups of three to five students (or smaller if resources permit). Students usually receive this supplemental instruction for 20 to 40 minutes per day, in addition to their regular classroom reading instruction, over a period of 10 to 30 weeks. Intervention is provided using specialized, scientifically based reading program(s)/curricula linked to students' instructional needs, and students' progress is monitored at least twice a month to ensure that they are on a trajectory to attain year-end benchmarks. In this chapter, we focus on secondary prevention using a standard protocol model within a three-tiered framework, in which as many as 20%–30% of students (depending on the effectiveness of the primary instruction) will require supplemental intervention.

How does secondary prevention (Tier 2) compare with tertiary intervention (Tier 3)? (In the next chapter, Fuchs, Stecker, and Fuchs will describe tertiary interventions in detail.) However, according to Reschly (2005), the primary differences in the tiers are with "intervention intensity and measurement precision" (p. 511). Secondary prevention and tertiary prevention can be compared on the basis of several important criteria: (a) students served in secondary interventions have less severe problems than students in tertiary interventions, (b) more intensive interventions are provided in tertiary programs, and (c) the expertise of individuals providing the intervention may vary, with teachers who are providing tertiary interventions demonstrating very high levels of expertise and knowledge. Two elements of intensity are duration of the intervention and group size, so tertiary interventions are provided for a more extended period per day in very small groups. Also, because students in tertiary interventions have the most severe difficulties and may be identified as learning disabled, the special education teacher or reading specialist provides the intervention. Specialized instruction that is adjusted to meet individual students' needs and that is modified as a result of ongoing progress monitoring is implemented.

What Are Some of the Key Considerations of a Secondary Intervention?

One important consideration when implementing secondary prevention is determining the resources needed in each particular educational setting. Related to the resources needed is the number of students at risk for reading problems. Students benefit when personnel are highly trained to implement the specified intervention. With this in mind, a range of personnel may provide secondary interventions, depending on the school or district practices and resources. Possible personnel include (a) classroom teachers who work cooperatively with other grade-level teachers to organize time each day to provide interventions, (b) certified teachers or reading specialists hired by the district to provide secondary interventions, or (c) highly trained and supervised paraprofessionals. Although most districts or schools might prefer that certified teachers provide secondary interventions, research indicates that intervention provided by well-trained tutors or paraprofessionals who are provided ongoing feedback and support is associated with improved outcomes for students (Elbaum, Vaughn, Hughes, & Moody, 2000; Grek, Mathes, & Torgesen, 2003). It should be noted that in cases where paraprofessionals or tutors are associated with improved outcomes, group sizes are very small (1:1 to 1:3). As districts and schools consider strategies for funding added personnel to provide secondary intervention, they may want to take advantage of the up to 15% of special education funds that the Individuals with Disabilities Education Act of 2004 stipulates can be used to implement prevention practices such as those provided through secondary intervention.

What Elements of Instruction Are Addressed Within Secondary Interventions?

Research suggests that there are identifiable elements of reading instruction associated with improved outcomes for students at risk for reading problems (McCardle & Chhabra, 2004; Snow, Burns & Griffin, 1998; Swanson & Hoskyn, 1999). The relative importance of each of these elements varies somewhat on the basis of the grade level and performance of the student. Tables 3.1, 3.2, and 3.3 provide a summary of the priority skills for each grade level for secondary interventions. In these figures, the key objectives and activities related to identifying priorities for secondary intervention for kindergarten students (Table 3.1), first-grade students (Table 3.2), and second- and third-grade students (Table 3.3) are described.

In addition to the broad guidelines provided in the figures, instructional practices are described for each element of reading.

TABLE 3.1

Kindergarten Reading Intervention Priorities

Instructional Component	Objective	Activities	Lesson Components
Phonological Awareness	• Students are able to manipulate onset and rimes (first semester) and phonemes (second semester) accurately and automatically	• Identify, blend, segment, and substitute words in sentences, syllables in words, onset/rime, phonemes with or without support	• Focus on one or two types of manipulation (e.g., blend and segment) • Start with activities that are oral initially, then link to print • Provide opportunities to respond individually and as a group • Can use manipulatives
Phonics and Word Study	• Students apply rules about how sounds are represented by letters • Students apply sound–symbol correspondences to read words accurately and fluently	• Identification of letter names and sounds, consonants in initial and final positions, also short vowels • Blending of sounds to read words • Dictation of letters and words	• Introduce letters and sounds systematically • Sounds are combined to form words • Give students opportunities to practice writing the letters and words they are learning
Listening Comprehension	• Students use comprehension strategies to interpret meaning from stories that have been read to them	• Narrative, expository read-alouds • Before reading: predicting and activating background knowledge • During reading: summarize periodically • After reading: questioning and retelling activities	• Introduce strategies systematically • Model strategies • Focus on most important idea • Use different types of questions

From Vaughn, S., & Linan-Thompson, S. (2004). *Research-Based Methods of Reading Instruction, Grades K–3*. Alexandria, VA: Association for Supervision and Curriculum Development. Adapted with permission. Learn more about ASCD at www.ascd.org.

TABLE 3.2

First-Grade Reading Intervention Priorities

Instructional Component	Objective	Activities	Lesson Components
Fluency	• Students automatically recognize words in isolation and in connected text	• Partner reading (student–adult or student–student) • Choral reading • Tape-assisted reading	• Provide a good, explicit model • Provide opportunities to reread text • Instruct students to reread text at least three times • Establish performance criteria
Phonological Awareness	• Students are able to manipulate phonemes	• Blending, segmenting of words at phoneme level with or without support	• Focus on one or two types of manipulation (e.g., blend and segment) • Use print • Provide opportunities to respond individually and as a group • Can use manipulatives
Phonics and Word Study	• Students apply sound–symbol correspondences to read words accurately and fluently • Students can use decoding strategies to read unknown words	• Blending of sounds to read words • Reading of decodable text • Word and sentence dictation	• Reading in books that contain words students have learned • Using decoding strategies • Patterns and rules are introduced systematically • Sounds are combined to form words
Comprehension	• Students use comprehension strategies before, during, and after reading text to construct meaning	• Engaging in comprehension strategies before, during, and after either having a text read to students or after reading a text • Predicting, activating background knowledge • Self-questioning, self-monitoring, answering and generating questions	• Model use of self-monitoring and comprehension strategies • Provide opportunities to use self-monitoring and comprehension strategies

From Vaughn, S., & Linan-Thompson, S. (2004). *Research-Based Methods of Reading Instruction, Grades K–3*. Alexandria, VA: Association for Supervision and Curriculum Development. Adapted with permission. Learn more about ASCD at www.ascd.org.

TABLE 3.3

Second- and Third-Grade Reading Intervention Priorities

Instructional Component	Objective	Activities	Lesson Components
Fluency	• Students recognize words automatically in connected text	• Partner reading (student–adult or student–student) • Choral reading • Tape-assisted reading • Fluency building at the word and phrase level	• Provide a good, explicit model • Provide opportunities to reread text • Instruct students to reread text at least three times • Establish performance criteria
Vocabulary	• Students use advanced word-recognition strategies when they encounter unknown words	• Teach words and their extended meaning systematically and continuously	• Model and teach the use of both explicit and implicit vocabulary instruction activities • Provide multiple opportunities to practice and use key vocabulary
Comprehension	• Students use comprehension strategies before, during, and after reading text to construct meaning • Students use self-monitoring strategies	• Before reading: prediction and activation of background knowledge • During reading: provide support in decoding, monitor comprehension • After reading: answering and generating questions, summarization	• Make sure book is at instructional level • Introduce book and preview vocabulary • Model use of self-monitoring and comprehension strategies • Provide opportunities to use self-monitoring and comprehension strategies

From Vaughn, S., & Linan-Thompson, S. (2004). *Research-Based Methods of Reading Instruction, Grades K–3*. Alexandria, VA: Association for Supervision and Curriculum Development. Adapted with permission. Learn more about ASCD at www.ascd.org.

When selecting or developing secondary interventions, it is critical to remember that in a relatively brief amount of time (typically 20–30 minutes for 10 to 20 weeks) we hope to have students "catch up" with their peers. For secondary interventions to be effective, instructional time during interventions needs to be highly focused and aligned with the primary instruction as well as the needs of the student. The extent to which each of these elements is emphasized is related to the student's instructional level.

Considering that the goal of secondary interventions is to close the performance gap with grade-level peers, how do educators provide secondary interventions with sufficient intensity to ensure that this occurs? Furthermore, secondary interventions need to be implemented within the "realities" of schools that are plagued by limited time and resources. How do we resolve the tension between students' needs and resource limitations? Two ways to provide sufficiently intensive interventions are to decrease the group size so that fewer students are with each teacher and to increase the amount of time for intervention. With respect to grouping practices, few teachers would deny that one-to-one instruction is the preferred instructional group size. However, few schools have resources to afford this level of intensity—particularly for secondary interventions. Thus, it is much more likely that schools will provide secondary interventions in group sizes of three to six students. There are several examples of studies in which students have responded positively to secondary intervention delivered in small groups (see, for example, Mathes et al., 2005; Vaughn & Linan-Thompson, 2003).

In addition to group size, interventions can be made more intensive by increasing the amount of time allotted for interventions per day, the number of days per week that interventions are provided, or both. Ultimately, schools will need to decide after 8–12 weeks of secondary intervention whether students are making adequate progress and whether their rates of progress on repeated progress monitoring assessments indicate that students are on a trajectory that will close the gap between their current performance and goal performance. Although there are many ways to provide secondary intervention, the most important issue to consider is whether the secondary intervention is intensive enough to provide students with a reasonable opportunity to "catch up" to grade-level expectations. It is also important to consider whether students are

provided secondary interventions for extensive periods of time and
denied opportunities for referral and placement in special education.

What Secondary Interventions Have Been Associated With Improved Outcomes for Students At Risk for Reading Difficulties?

There are numerous examples of standard protocol interventions
associated with improved outcomes for students who are
monolingual English readers (e.g., Felton, 1993; Foorman, 2003;
Kamps & Greenwood, 2005; Mathes et al., 2005; Torgesen et al., 1999;
Torgesen et al., 2001; Vellutino et al., 1996) as well as for students
who are English-language learners (e.g., Vaughn, Cirino, et al., 2006;
Vaughn, Linan–Thompson, et al., 2006). In addition to the key
elements of instruction summarized in Tables 3.1–3.3, students
benefit from interventions that

- Use appropriate grouping formats
- Provide targeted instruction three to five times per week
- Ensure additional instruction aligns with students' primary reading instruction
- Provide ongoing and systematic instruction with feedback and scaffolded instructional support to students
- Provide extended practice in the critical components of reading instruction based on students' needs
- Increase time as needed for word study, fluency, and comprehension
- Use systematic curriculum-based assessment to document student growth and inform instruction

Table 3.4 provides guidelines for implementing effective
secondary prevention in schools. Several key ideas are linked to

TABLE 3.4

Guidelines for Implementing Effective Secondary Intervention

Implement universal screening to identify students at risk for reading problems.	• Develop procedures for screening all students at least twice a year (beginning of year and middle of year) to determine students at risk for reading problems. Provide students at risk with appropriate interventions.
Determine students' instructional needs.	• Determine students' knowledge and skills related to relevant reading elements expected at their grade level (e.g., phonemic awareness, alphabet knowledge, phonics, word reading, word or text fluency, vocabulary, spelling, and comprehension).
Form same-ability, small groups.	• For secondary intervention, form groups of students with similar learning needs. Group sizes should be as small as local resources will allow.
Provide daily, targeted instruction that is explicit, systematic, and that provides ample practice opportunities with immediate feedback.	• Identify the instructional content in small instructional units (e.g., three to five minutes per unit) for each lesson. • Focus on the reading skills that have the highest impact on learning to read based on students' current performance. • Provide modeled examples before student practice. • Follow a systematic routine. Use clear, explicit, easy-to-follow procedures. • Sequence instruction so that easier reading skills are introduced before more complex ones. • Pace instruction quickly so students are engaged and content is covered. • Maximize student engagement, including many opportunities for students to respond. • Provide immediate positive and corrective feedback. • Provide ample opportunities for guided initial practice and independent practice. • Monitor student understanding and mastery of instruction frequently. • Scaffold instruction and make adaptations to instruction in response to students' needs and to how quickly or slowly students are learning. • Adapt instruction so that items are more difficult for some students and easier for other students. • Include frequent and cumulative reviews of previously learned material. • Reteach, when necessary.

(continued)

TABLE 3.4 (continued)

Guidelines for Implementing Effective Secondary Intervention

Ensure that students are reading texts at the appropriate level of difficulty.	• Independent level: Texts in which no more than approximately 1 in 20 words is read incorrectly (accuracy level: 95%–100%). • Instructional level: Texts in which no more than approximately 1 in 10 words is read incorrectly. Students need instructional support from the teacher (accuracy level: 90%–94%). • Frustration level: Texts in which more than 1 in 10 words is read incorrectly (accuracy level: less than 90%). • Reading accuracy levels vary from source to source. To calculate reading accuracy, divide the number of words read correctly by the total number of words read.
Match reading levels to the purpose for reading.	• When students are reading text independently without teacher (or peer) guidance and support, levels of accuracy need to be very high. When students are reading text with teacher guidance and support, lower levels of accuracy may be appropriate.
Provide many opportunities for struggling readers to apply phonics and word study learning to reading words, word lists, and connected texts.	• Have students practice reading words and texts at the appropriate level of difficulty (usually instructional level under the direction of the teacher). • Include the reading of word cards or words in phrases or sentences to increase word recognition fluency (often used with high-frequency and irregular words and words that contain previously taught letter–sound correspondences or spelling patterns). • Include comprehension instruction that introduces new vocabulary words, incorporates graphic organizers, and teaches comprehension strategies explicitly.
Include writing to support reading and spelling.	• Have students apply what they are learning about letters and sounds as they write letters, sound units, words, and sentences. • Involve parents so they support students' efforts by listening to them read and practicing reading skills. • Conduct frequent progress monitoring (e.g., every one to two weeks) to track student progress and inform instruction and grouping.

From University of Texas Center for Reading and Language Arts (2004). *Implementing the 3-Tier Reading Model: Reducing reading difficulties for kindergarten through third grade students.* Austin, TX: Author. Adapted with permission. Based on Gunning, 2002; Morrow, 2001; Texas Governor's Business Council, 2000; Torgesen et al., 2001; & University of Texas Center for Reading and Language Arts, 2002.

improved outcomes for students with reading difficulties: (a) explicit and well-organized instruction; (b) frequent cumulative review of previously mastered content; (c) self-regulation strategies that promote students monitoring their own academic progress and goal setting; (d) peer instruction, mediation, and support for extending instruction; and (e) a focus on higher order processing.

How Do Educators Know Whether Students Are Responding Adequately to Secondary Interventions?

Assessment practices for determining whether students are adequately progressing toward their instructional goals are essential to effective implementation of RTI. Students receiving secondary intervention are likely to fall within one of three broad categories (McMaster, Fuchs, Fuchs, & Compton, 2005; Vaughn, Linan-Thompson, & Hickman, 2003; Vellutino, Scanlon, & Lyon, 2000): (1) adequate progress toward their goals, (2) inadequate progress toward their goals, (3) limited progress toward their goals. The majority of students who are provided secondary intervention make adequate progress after 50–100 sessions of intervention. A student making adequate progress and who reaches his or her instructional goal is no longer in the "risk" category for reading problems and can profit from primary classroom instruction without intervention. Some students make progress, but the progress made is inadequate for them to reach their instructional goal and to profit from primary instruction alone. These students do not make enough progress to "catch up" with grade-level expectations for reading performance. A minority (fewer than 10% of all secondary intervention students) make little or no substantial progress.

> **The majority of students who are provided secondary intervention make adequate progress after 50–100 sessions of intervention.**

Having timely and reliable information on students' progress in classroom instruction and secondary intervention is critical. Consider the three groups of students discussed in the previous paragraph. The first group, students whose response to secondary intervention is adequate, consists of students who are making progress toward their reading goals. There are two essential decisions regarding these students: (1) continue students in secondary intervention because while they are making progress they still require additional intervention or (2) determine whether students are candidates for discontinuation from secondary intervention, though it will be prudent to continue monitoring their response to classroom instruction to assure that they do not require secondary intervention at a later time.

The second group, students making inadequate progress toward their goals, may benefit from continuing in the secondary intervention—if evidence supports continuation—or these students may require an alternative instructional program or referral to special education.

Students in the third group, those making limited progress, require consideration of the following questions:

- Is a more intensive intervention required—perhaps additional instructional time or reduced group size?

- Is a different or modified instructional curriculum/program needed?

- Are the special needs of the student addressed?

The answers to these important questions are based on data from progress monitoring assessments (Vaughn & Fuchs, 2003). These measures, which are directly linked to instruction, are administered at regular intervals throughout an instructional sequence, enabling a teacher to track students' progress in key skills over time (Deno, Fuchs, Marston, & Shin, 2001). Teachers can use information from progress monitoring assessments to determine whether students' rate of growth is on a trajectory to enable them to reach grade-level benchmarks. Progress monitoring assessments are unique in that they are simply and quickly administered, can be administered repeatedly within a relatively narrow time period, and yield almost immediate results. In addition, these measures are very sensitive to small changes in student performance, allowing teachers to observe whether adjustments to instruction (such

as providing more explicit instruction with increased opportunities for practice) result in accelerated student progress. Importantly, progress monitoring measures can allow teachers to observe even small increments of growth. Awareness of this progress can be highly motivating to teachers of struggling readers and to the students themselves. Well-designed progress monitoring measures provide reliable and relevant information for making instructional decisions and for refining instructional plans (Marston, Mirkin, & Deno, 1984).

Fuchs (2003) identifies three primary considerations when planning and implementing a system of progress monitoring:

1. As a rule, progress monitoring measures are closely aligned with instruction; what is measured and what is taught are linked. For early reading instruction, for example, measures of phonemic awareness, letter–sound correspondence, word identification, phonemic decoding, and text-reading fluency are appropriate. Evidence suggests that simple measures of oral reading fluency can provide reliable information about primary-grade students' growth in word-reading skills and that measures of fluency are also good indicators of primary-grade students' reading comprehension (Fuchs, Fuchs, Hosp, & Jenkins, 2001).

2. Students with severe reading difficulties are monitored more frequently (every week or two) than less impaired readers (every two to three weeks). Students who appear to be developing

readers and students who respond quickly to secondary intervention are monitored three to four times a year to identify those who need subsequent intervention.

3. Decisions about students' adequate or inadequate response to intervention are made on the basis of well-developed progress monitoring measures. Teacher-developed measures are useful to inform instruction, but they may lack the necessary precision to accurately identify students' RTI. Because of the serious consequences of mistakes in deciding whether a student has responded inadequately to secondary intervention and thus requires extended secondary or highly intensive tertiary intervention, progress monitoring measures used in RTI models must be of high quality.

What Are Some Issues With Secondary Intervention?

There are two determinants of students' success in reading—quality of instruction and opportunity to learn (Gerber, 2005). Effective secondary interventions address both of these elements. However, there are some challenges to implementing secondary interventions effectively. Perhaps the greatest challenge to effectively implementing secondary interventions is ensuring that highly qualified personnel are available to "scale up" the interventions that have been effectively implemented in research studies. Scaling up refers to spreading the use of practices that were effectively implemented in controlled settings to broader use in other school settings. The "scaling up" of these standardized secondary interventions in natural settings is associated with positive effects (Denton, Vaughn, & Fletcher, 2003); however, the procedures are not easy to implement, and many schools will be challenged to establish the necessary procedures and practices to implement secondary interventions effectively.

Another essential issue to consider is that the number of students requiring secondary interventions is directly related to the quality of classroom-based primary (Tier 1) instruction provided (Kamps & Greenwood, 2005). Schools in which all teachers implement high-quality research-based primary instruction will have reduced numbers of students requiring secondary intervention.

In addition, school leadership is essential to effective implementation of primary and secondary instructional practices. Knowledgeable and supportive leaders who serve as curriculum guides are a critical component. Effectively implementing and sustaining secondary interventions requires that school leaders are committed to prevention-oriented practices; are willing to assure that scientifically based research practices are implemented; ensure that secondary intervention teachers receive high-quality, ongoing professional development; and are committed to the use of ongoing assessments to determine student progress and adjust instructional decisions.

> **School leadership is essential to effective implementation of primary and secondary instructional practices.**

Conclusion

Providing effective secondary interventions for students at risk for reading problems holds considerable promise for reducing reading difficulties. However, there are no simple or easy solutions. Students with reading difficulties have heterogeneous needs that require capable and thoughtful instructional planning, quality instruction, and frequent progress monitoring to inform instruction. Students make gains specifically related to what is taught and benefit from an integrated curriculum that links secondary intervention with primary instruction. Decision making related to secondary interventions needs to be provided by knowledgeable and experienced professionals who consider the feasibility of implementation within the general education context. Essential to effective secondary intervention is ongoing screening and progress monitoring to assure that students with reading difficulties are readily identified and that their RTI is monitored regularly.

REFERENCES

Batsche, G., Elliott, J., Graden, J.L., Grimes, J., Kovaleski, J.F., Prasse, D., et al. (2005). *Response to intervention: Policy considerations and implementation.* Alexandria, VA: National Association of State Directors of Special Education.

Deno, S.L., Fuchs, L.S., Marston, D., & Shin, J. (2001). Using curriculum-based measurement to establish growth standards for students with learning disabilities. *School Psychology Review, 30*(4), 507–524.

Denton, C.A., Vaughn, S., & Fletcher, J.M. (2003). Bringing researched-based practice in reading intervention to scale. *Learning Disabilities: Research & Practice, 18*(3), 201–211.

Elbaum, B., Vaughn, S., Hughes, M.T., & Moody, S.W. (2000). How effective are one-to-one tutoring programs in reading for elementary students at risk for reading failure? A meta-analysis of the intervention research. *Journal of Educational Psychology, 92*(4), 605–619.

Felton, R. (1993). Effects of instruction on the decoding skills of children with phonological-processing problems. *Journal of Learning Disabilities, 26*(9), 583–589.

Foorman, B.R. (Ed.). (2003). *Preventing and remediating reading difficulties: Bringing science to scale.* Timonium, MD: York Press.

Fuchs, L.S. (2003). Assessing intervention responsiveness: Conceptual and technical issues. *Learning Disabilities Research & Practice, 18*(3), 172–186.

Fuchs, L.S., Fuchs, D., Hosp, M.K., & Jenkins, J.R. (2001). Oral reading fluency as an indicator of reading competence: A theoretical, empirical, and historical analysis. *Scientific Studies of Reading, 5*(3), 239–256.

Gerber, M.M. (2005). Teachers are still the test: Limitations of response to instruction strategies for identifying children with learning disabilities. *Journal of Learning Disabilities, 38*(6), 516–524.

Grek, M.L., Mathes, P.G., & Torgesen, J.K. (2003). Similarities and differences between experienced teachers and trained paraprofessionals: An observational analysis. In S. Vaughn & K.L. Briggs (Eds.), *Reading in the classroom: Systems for the observation of teaching and learning* (pp. 267–296). Baltimore: Brookes.

Gunning, T.G. (2002). *Assessing and correcting reading and writing difficulties* (2nd ed.). Boston: Allyn & Bacon.

Hasbrouck, J., & Denton, C.A. (2005). *The reading coach: A how-to manual for success.* Longmont, CO: Sopris West.

Kamps, D.M., & Greenwood, C.R. (2005). Formulating secondary-level reading interventions. *Journal of Learning Disabilities, 38*(6), 500–509.

Marston, D., Mirkin, P., & Deno, S.L. (1984). Curriculum-based measurement: An alternative to traditional screening, referral, and identification. *The Journal of Special Education, 18*(2), 109–117.

Mathes, P.G., Denton, C.A., Fletcher, J.M., Anthony, J.L., Francis, D.J., & Schatschneider, C. (2005). The effects of theoretically different instruction and student characteristics on the skills of struggling readers. *Reading Research Quarterly, 40*(2), 148–182.

McCardle, P., & Chhabra, V. (Eds.). (2004). *The voice of evidence in reading research.* Baltimore: Brookes.

McMaster, K.L.N., Fuchs, D., Fuchs, L.S., & Compton, D.L. (2005). Responding to nonresponders: An experimental field trial of identification and intervention methods. *Exceptional Children, 71*(4), 445–463.

Morrow, L.M. (2001). *Literacy development in the early years: Helping children read and write* (4th ed.). Boston: Allyn & Bacon.

Reschly, D. (2005). Learning disabilities identification: Primary intervention, secondary intervention, and then what? *Journal of Learning Disabilities, 38*(6), 510–515.

Snow, C.E., Burns, M.S., & Griffin, P. (Eds.). (1998). *Preventing reading difficulties in young children.* Washington, DC: National Academy Press.

Swanson, H.L., & Hoskyn, M. (1999). Definition x treatment interactions for students with learning disabilities. *School Psychology Review, 28*(4), 644–658.

Texas Governor's Business Council. (2000). *How do I know a good reading intervention when I see one?* [Brochure]. Austin, TX: Author.

Torgesen, J.K., Alexander, A.W., Wagner, R.K., Rashotte, C.A., Voeller, K., Conway, T., et al. (2001). Intensive remedial instruction for children with severe reading disabilities: Immediate and long-term outcomes from two instructional approaches. *Journal of Learning Disabilities, 34*(1), 33–58, 78.

Torgesen, J.K., Wagner, R.K., Rashotte, C.A., Rose, E., Lindamood, P., Conway, T., et al. (1999). Preventing reading failure in young children with phonological processing disabilities: Group and individual responses to instruction. *Journal of Educational Psychology, 91*(4), 579–593.

University of Texas Center for Reading and Language Arts. (2002). *Second grade teacher reading academy.* Austin, TX: Author.

University of Texas Center for Reading and Language Arts. (2004). *Implementing the 3-Tier Reading Model: Reducing reading difficulties for kindergarten through third grade students.* Austin, TX: Author.

Vaughn, S., Cirino, P.T., Linan-Thompson, S., Mathes, P.G., Carlson, C.D., Cardenas-Hagan, E., et al. (2006). Effectiveness of a Spanish intervention and an English intervention for English-language learners at risk for reading problems. *American Educational Research Journal, 43*(3), 449–487.

Vaughn, S., & Fuchs, L.S. (2003). Redefining learning disabilities as inadequate response to instruction: The promise and potential problems. *Learning Disabilities Research & Practice, 18*(3), 137–146.

Vaughn, S., & Linan-Thompson, S. (2003). Group size and time allotted to intervention: Effects for students with reading difficulties. In B. Foorman (Ed.), *Preventing and remediating reading difficulties: Bringing science to scale* (pp. 299–324). Timonium, MD: York Press.

Vaughn, S., & Linan-Thompson, S. (2004). *Research-based methods of reading instruction: Grades K–3.* Alexandria, VA: Association for Supervision and Curriculum Development.

Vaughn, S., Linan-Thompson, S., & Hickman, P. (2003). Response to instruction as a means of identifying students with reading/learning disabilities. *Exceptional Children, 69*(4), 391–409.

Vaughn, S., Linan-Thompson, S., Mathes, P.G., Cirino, P.T., Carlson, C.D., Pollard-Durodola, S.D., et al. (2006). Effectiveness of Spanish intervention for first-grade English language learners at risk for reading difficulties. *Journal of Learning Disabilities, 39*(1), 56–73.

Vellutino, F.R., Scanlon, D.M., & Lyon, G.R. (2000). Differentiating between difficult-to-remediate and readily remediated poor readers: More evidence against the IQ-achievement discrepancy definition of reading disability. *Journal of Learning Disabilities, 33*(3), 223–238.

Vellutino, F.R., Scanlon, D.M., Sipay, E.R., Small, S.G., Pratt, A., Chen, R., et al. (1996). Cognitive profiles of difficult-to-remediate and readily remediated poor readers: Early intervention as a vehicle for distinguishing between cognitive and experiential deficits as basic causes of specific reading disability. *Journal of Educational Psychology, 88*(4), 601–638.

Tier 3: Why Special Education Must Be the Most Intensive Tier in a Standards-Driven, No Child Left Behind World

Douglas Fuchs, Pamela M. Stecker, and Lynn S. Fuchs

I n August 2006, the U.S. Department of Education published its much anticipated regulations to accompany the 2004 reauthorization of Individuals With Disabilities Education Improvement Act (Public Law 108–446; IDEA 2004). Many had waited impatiently for the document to clarify Responsiveness-to-Instruction (RTI), an alternative method of identifying children with learning disabilities (LD), legitimized as such in the 2004 reauthorization of IDEA. When finally published, virtually all interested parties were disappointed in the regulations. They underspecified RTI and created widespread confusion and anxiety, a situation that continues today.

What Is RTI?

Despite the weak official guidance—on formal definitions of purpose and procedure—there is growing consensus that RTI is meant to

provide earlier intervention and prevention and more valid disability identification. Many also seem to agree in principle that it starts with the teacher providing scientifically validated, or "generally effective," instruction; identifying at-risk students; and monitoring their academic progress. Those students who do not respond to classroom instruction get something else or something more from the teacher, reading coach, or someone else. Again, progress is monitored. Students responsive to the more intensive instruction return to the classroom, where practitioners continue to monitor their performance. Students who are unresponsive either qualify for special education by virtue of their unresponsiveness or are provided a comprehensive evaluation to determine special education eligibility, depending on the version of RTI. Where chronic unresponsiveness is the necessary and sufficient condition for special education eligibility (e.g., Heartland, Iowa, Area Education Agency and Minneapolis Public Schools), practitioners use a "low-achievement" definition of disability (e.g., Ikeda & Gustafson, 2002; Minneapolis Public Schools, 2001), circumventing controversial issues like whether and how to measure students' learning potential.

RTI should also provide help more quickly to a greater number of struggling students (e.g., Grimes, 2002; Lyon et al., 2001). A related expectation is that by providing more intensive instruction to these students, RTI distinguishes poorly performing children with disabilities from those who perform poorly because of inadequate instruction (cf. Compton, Fuchs, Fuchs, & Bryant, 2006; Fuchs, Fuchs, & Compton, 2004; Vellutino et al., 1996). A successful separation of "true positives" (i.e., those truly disabled) from "false positives" (i.e., those who appear disabled but are not) is an important step toward reducing special education enrollments and costs (e.g., Batsche et al., 2005).

RTI, then, should encourage serious and sustained early intervention with at-risk students, leading to stronger school performance and to fewer special education referrals, all of which enhances the validity of the disability-identification process. Such changes in service delivery would be of substantial benefit to students, teachers, and schools. At the same time, important questions are being asked about (a) whether teachers will indeed implement scientifically validated instruction with fidelity; (b) whether teachers and their support staff will correctly identify at-risk students—those likely to be unresponsive to "first-tier" instruction—and will choose valid measures to regularly monitor their academic progress; (c) whether school districts will deploy more intensive, best-evidence, "second-tier" instruction for students unresponsive to first-tier instruction; (d) whether the students' performance will be monitored at this second tier and, for those deemed responsive enough to return to the classroom, whether practitioners will continue to monitor the students' performance there; and (e) whether these many activities will lead to reductions in special education enrollments and cost.

More Basic Questions About RTI

How Many Tiers Make Up the RTI Framework?

There are more fundamental questions (cf. Fuchs & Deshler, 2007; Gerber, 2003; Mastropieri & Scruggs, 2005) to address. One involves the number of instructional tiers in RTI, with some arguing for as few as two or three and others promoting four, five, or more. The number of tiers one favors can be a window on one's thoughts about RTI's primary purpose: Disability identification or early intervention and prevention? Those who see RTI as mainly about disability identification want fewer tiers. Those who see RTI primarily in terms of early intervention and prevention want more tiers. Those favoring fewer tiers tend also to prefer a conventional or traditional version of special education, whereas many who promote the use of more tiers advocate for a very different special education.

Is the Purpose of RTI Disability Idenitification or Early Intervention?

Fewer tiers serve disability identification better than more tiers because with more tiers practitioners inadvertently increase the likelihood of identifying false negatives—that is, students who truly need special education but appear not to need it. This is because more tiers will provide more intensive treatments; treatments with an intensity (e.g., greater duration, instructional expertise, group homogeneity) equaling or exceeding the intensity of special education instruction. Such a circumstance raises the question, How will practitioners interpret the performance of a nonresponsive student who finally responds to instruction, say, in a fourth or fifth tier? Is this student now helped sufficiently so she's ready to return to the regular classroom, or does her responsiveness to instruction at this most intensive tier mean that she is an appropriate candidate for special education? If sent back to the regular class, will she likely continue to improve academically or will she become once more a nonresponder? Many believe she would be a candidate for special education and returning her to the regular classroom would inadvertently deprive her of her rights to an appropriate education defined in IDEA 2004.

Advocates of more tiers see RTI primarily as a means of making general education more muscular; more strongly oriented to early intervention and prevention; more capable of accommodating a greater academic diversity of children. Recent changes in IDEA 2004 give general educators 15% of federal special education dollars, the purpose of which is to "front-load" these monies to develop more tiers and strengthen early intervention and prevention.

Should Special Education Be Conventional or Unconventional?

Whether one thinks of RTI in terms of fewer tiers or more tiers also reveals a preference for conventional or unconventional versions of special education. Those supporting fewer tiers see special education in conventional or traditional terms: existing for only chronically unresponsive students and existing outside the tier structure, or as a last tier, in which special educators use curricula, materials, and instruction and progress monitoring strategies that may differ from those used by instructors in preceding tiers and apply an intensity of effort unequaled in general education. Fewer tiers mean students get special education more quickly. Implicit is the confidence that it is generally a "good" service to be accessed, not a "bad" one to be avoided. This view contrasts with those who hold that special education is generally an undesirable service option and that a greater number of tiers can help more students avoid it. See for example a recent article on RTI in *The Wall Street Journal* (Tomsho, 2007), in which Daniel Reschly is quoted as saying that early intervention is more humane than special education.

Many who argue for more tiers envision a very different special education: One that is part of—rather than apart from—the general education tiers. They prefer a deliberate "blurring" of special and general education (cf. McLaughlin, 2006; National Association of State Directors of Special Education/Council of Administrators of Special Education [NASDSE/CASE], 2006), with special education folded into each of the tiers, presumably making them more effective for a greater number of students with and without disabilities. In such a service delivery system, described below as a new "continuum of general education placements and services," special education is no longer a *place* like a resource room or self-contained classroom in a school building, but rather a *service* brought to students in whatever general education tier they happen

> Special education is no longer a *place* like a resource room or self-contained classroom in a school building, but rather a *service* brought to students in whatever general education tier they happen to be.

to be. To create a context for a discussion of this new continuum of general education placements and services, we first describe the more established special education continuum.

Special Education and General Education: A "Traditional" vs. "New" Continuum of Placements and Services

The "Traditional" Continuum

Also known as "the cascade of services" (Deno, 1970; Reynolds, 1962), the continuum of special education placements and services has been the backbone of special education service delivery since written into Public Law 94-142 (a.k.a. "Education for All Handicapped Children's Act" of 1975). Its most important purpose is to ensure an appropriate education for all children identified with a disability. An appropriate educational placement must pass muster on two counts: It must address the student's unique learning and social needs and occur in a setting as close as possible to students without disabilities. Only a placement satisfying both criteria may be recognized as a "least restrictive environment." Whereas IDEA 2004 requires practitioners to regard the mainstream classroom as the presumptive placement for all students with disabilities, the law also recognizes that this will not be every student's least restrictive environment. (See, for example, a recent Supreme Court decision [Board of Education of New York City v. Tom F.; Case No. 06-637] that upholds a ruling by the U.S. Court of Appeals for the 2nd Circuit, in New York City, that IDEA does not require children to have attended public schools before their parents can seek reimbursement for a "unilateral" private placement [Schemo & Medina, 2007; Walsh, 2007].)

Hence, IDEA 2004 demands school districts to provide a continuum of special education to general education placements. At one end is the mainstream classroom, a setting that guarantees physical proximity to typically developing students. At the other end is the student's home or an institution, which most often precludes contact with nondisabled students. It is assumed that as a student moves from the mainstream classroom toward resource rooms, self-contained classes, "special" (i.e., separate) day schools, and so forth, instruction becomes increasingly specialized and intensive. IDEA 2004, in keeping with prior reauthorizations of the law, requires stakeholders to balance this intensity of services necessary for students' appropriate education against their need to be as proximal as possible to typically developing peers.

© 2008 JupiterImages Corporation

Critics of the "Traditional" Continuum

In the mid-to-late 1980s and early 1990s, a group of advocates for children with severe intellectual disabilities tried to dismantle the special education continuum of placements and services and promote the general education classroom as the *only* legitimate educational placement for all children (e.g., Gartner & Lipsky, 1987; Pearpoint & Forest, 1992; Stainback & Stainback, 1992; Taylor, 1988; Thousand & Villa, 1990). The crux of their full-inclusion-for-all position was (a) that the technical know-how (i.e., the instructional strategies, curricula, and materials) already existed to make regular classrooms sufficiently accommodating of all students, including those with the most severe disabilities; (b) that eliminating the special education continuum of placements would create the necessary monies to ensure that all schools could afford this technical

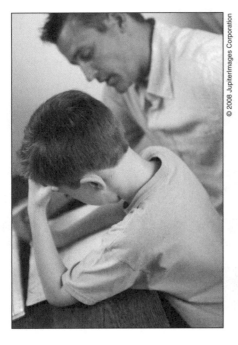
© 2008 Jupiterimages Corporation

know-how and would also unleash specialists of all kinds (e.g., physical and occupational therapists, speech clinicians, special educators) to work with students with and without disabilities in the regular classroom; and (c) that it was morally indefensible *not* to work toward this transformation. Implicit in the full-inclusion position was that, for most children with so-called high-incidence disabilities (i.e., LD, behavior disorders, and mild mental retardation) the move from special education to general education would be relatively easy and successful because a majority of these students had disabilities that were easily accommodated or, perhaps, they were not really disabled.

More recently, McLaughlin (2006) has been explicit on this last point. She writes that many consider students with LD, behavior disorders, and mild mental retardation labels to be products of a general education system that has failed "to adequately support individual differences" (p. 18). Although she allows that most of these children perform very poorly in school, she argues that (a) they are not disabled and don't require "vastly different and highly specialized curriculum or instruction" (p. 20); (b) their "disabilities" are little more than social constructions (p. 18); and (c) the 6.6 million children currently served by special education across the nation (cf. National Center for Education Statistics, 2005) may be reduced by 75% (McLaughlin, 2006, p. 31) to 1.65 million, or from 13% of the general population to 3.25%.

The "New" Continuum

If, as McLaughlin (2006) argues, the ranks of special needs students swelled because of general education's incapacity to accommodate them in the first place, what now will make general education more accommodating? McLaughlin's answer seems to come in two parts. First, it reflects her basic support of the full-inclusion position expressed two decades ago, as already discussed. Second, she believes important remedies for general education are in recent federal legislation; namely, "standards-driven" reform. Begun with the 1994 reauthorization of Title 1 of the Elementary and Secondary Education Act (ESEA), and strengthened in the 2001 reauthorization of ESEA (a.k.a. No Child Left Behind Act), standards-driven reform, she writes, dominates educational policy today. A standards-driven approach assumes that uniformly challenging standards are established for all students; assessments are aligned with those standards; virtually all students (including most students with disabilities) participate in these assessments at least annually; and the students' performance on these tests becomes the basis for district-level and school-level accountability. McLaughlin says such an approach is meant primarily to close the achievement gap between traditionally enfranchised and disenfranchised student groups. Included among the groups targeted by the standards-driven No Child Left Behind Act are special needs students. In short, McLaughlin states that standards-driven reforms, expressed with increasing clarity and conviction in a succession of federal documents for more than a decade, make it clear that most children currently identified as disabled will become nondisabled with the "right" general education in place (p. 20).

And the right general education—apart from challenging standards, regular assessments aligned with the standards, and accountability based on student outcomes—will be characterized by a new continuum of general education placements and services. The placements will be RTI tiers; the services will be the increasingly intensive instruction across the tiers, made possible in part by the closing of resource rooms and self-contained classrooms and redeployment of special educators as coteachers in Tier 1, small-group tutors in Tier 2, and so forth. In other words, for McLaughlin and others (e.g., Elliott, 2007; Hardman, 2007; NASDSE/CASE, 2006), RTI becomes an important operationalization of a standards-driven vision for both a reconfigured special education and reinvigorated general education.

Skepticism About Whether the "New" Continuum Will Take Hold

Despite her enthusiasm for what we are calling a new general education continuum of placements and services, McLaughlin (2006) is skeptical that states and districts will implement it. Her doubt is caused by what she refers to as a "culture of special education," which she sees as a formidable obstacle. An important feature of this putative culture is its alleged hostility to standards. McLaughlin writes that this culture assumes that

> a child with a disability will require *individualized* education...tailored to [the] disability [italics in the original]. The unit of improvement is the child and the improvement is individually referenced. Special education [culture] does not assume that providing [special education]...will move a child to some absolute standard or to alter the disability which is seen as a fixed condition. (p. 22)

In addition, because of special education's misguided emphasis on individualized instruction and Individualized Education Programs (IEP), "aggregate performance data is impossible to obtain, privacy provisions prevent open scrutiny of student progress or attainment of goals" (p. 11), and there are no consequences associated with students' failure to obtain their goals.

Why Special Education Must Be RTI's Final Tier

We, too, are skeptical about an approach that eliminates the special education continuum of placements and subsumes much of its services within the tiers of a new general education continuum. However, our reasons are different from McLaughlin's. First, we believe she overestimates the number of children currently labeled "disabled" who can be accommodated by general education's new continuum of placements and services. Our view is based on several of the same RTI studies she invokes in arguing for a new continuum. Across many of these investigations (e.g., McMaster, Fuchs, Fuchs, & Compton, 2005; Torgesen, 2000), researchers have independently estimated the proportion of chronic nonresponders—those whose academic performance is not improved by increasingly intensive instruction across tiers—to be the equivalent of 2% to 6% of the general population. This estimated range is only for students with LD; it does not account for children with behavior disorders, mild mental retardation, autism, language disorders, and other disabilities. Further, researchers in many of these studies conducted very intensive treatments; that is, many sessions across months and sometimes years that were implemented with fidelity by expert instructors. Which raises this question: How likely would school-based practitioners implement equally intensive treatments with the same strong fidelity? Our answer: not likely.

An important implication is that when RTI is implemented by teachers, school psychologists, reading teachers, and others at the building level, we can anticipate the proportion of nonresponders to be greater than the proportion reported by researchers. Although we recognize that numerous students are currently identified incorrectly as disabled, and we view this situation as unacceptable, we believe it is unrealistic to think that schools using a new general education continuum of placements and services (i.e., RTI) can reduce the special needs population by 75% or any number approaching 75%. Assuming practitioners implement RTI with fidelity, we predict at least 6% to 8% of the general population (i.e., 3 million to 4 million children) will require special education services, or between two and three times the number estimated by McLaughlin. Of course, whether we're right or McLaughlin is right is a matter for research. "It's an empirical question," as we say, and currently there is no answer.

Second, McLaughlin's (2006) and others' description of instruction in a new continuum is incomplete on three important counts. She does not recognize how little differentiated instruction presently occurs in general education, how few practices implemented in the name of differentiated instruction are evidence based, and that there will be many nonresponders to evidence-based instruction.

The Absence of Differentiated Education

There is persuasive evidence that most classrooms are bereft of differentiated instruction. For example, Baker and Zigmond (1990) conducted interviews and observations in reading and math classes in an elementary school to explore whether teachers implement routine adaptations (e.g., differentiating instruction by creating multiple reading groups to accommodate weak-to-strong readers at the start of the school year). Baker and Zigmond found no evidence of routine adaptations. Rather, they reported that teachers typically taught to large groups, using lessons incorporating little or no differentiation on the basis of student needs. McIntosh, Vaughn, Schumm, Haager, and Lee (1994) described similar results from their observations of 60 social studies and science classrooms across grades 3 to 12. Moreover, findings from numerous studies document that many low-achieving students, including those with special needs, not only fail to obtain differentiated instruction in mainstream classrooms but receive less *undifferentiated* instruction and practice than their more accomplished classmates (e.g., Delquadri, Greenwood, Whorton, Carta, & Hall, 1986; Hall, Delquadri, Greenwood, & Thurston, 1982; Lesgold & Resnick, 1982; McDermott & Aron, 1978; O'Sullivan, Ysseldyke, Christenson, & Thurlow, 1990). Those who argue for a new

> **There is persuasive evidence that most classrooms are bereft of differentiated instruction.**

continuum of general education placements and services are optimistic about general education's capacity to accommodate most students, including most students currently identified as requiring special education, despite general education's dismal record on this point.

Limitations of Evidence-Based Efforts to Differentiate Instruction and Accommodate Students With Disabilities

Best practices developed during the past 20 years have included cooperative learning (e.g., Johnson & Johnson, 1994); Success For All, (e.g., Slavin & Madden, 2000, 2003); Direct Instruction (e.g., Carnine, Silbert, Kame'enui, & Tarver, 2004); peer tutoring programs such as Peer-Assisted Learning Strategies (e.g., Fuchs & Fuchs, 2005) and Classwide Peer Tutoring (e.g., Delquadri et al., 1986; Greenwood, Delquadri, & Hall, 1989); self-regulated strategy instruction (e.g., De La Paz, Owen, Harris, & Graham, 2000; Deshler et al., 2001), and curriculum-based measurement (CBM; e.g., Deno, 1985; Fuchs & Fuchs, 1986). Without attempting to diminish these important accomplishments, it is noteworthy that best practices typically represent only modest attempts to differentiate instruction. Few developers of best practices recognize that some students will not benefit from them even when they are implemented faithfully, and what these students require is a validated variant of the practice or a research-backed supplement to it. Thus, it should not be surprising that, whereas a majority of students benefit from best practices when implemented with strong fidelity, many do not Cooperative learning is a case in point.

Cooperative learning, when used appropriately, can benefit many students. Positive academic and social outcomes have been reported for typically developing students in every major subject area, at all grade levels, and in many types of schools worldwide.

Nevertheless, researchers have reported mixed results in studies in which it was used to improve the academic achievement of students with disabilities. In a recent review of this literature, McMaster and Fuchs (2002) found that, among the 15 studies meeting their inclusion criteria, only 6 studies reported cooperative learning to reliably promote special needs students' achievement beyond controls' achievement (see their Table 1, pp. 109–110). This finding underscores the well-known fact that, irrespective of the general effectiveness of a given curriculum or instructional program or procedure, there will inevitably be nonresponders.

McLaughlin (2006) and others promote coteaching as another evidence-based practice for differentiating instruction in general education classrooms to accommodate most children with disabilities. Nevertheless, there is meager empirical support for this claim (cf. Murawski & Swanson, 2001; Scruggs, Mastropieri, & McDuffie, 2007; Zigmond, 2006; Zigmond & Baker, 1994; Zigmond & Matta, 2005). Indeed, its evidence base is considerably *less* than that which supports cooperative learning. Which prompts the question, Who will teach the many nonresponders who inevitably will emerge in a given school building where the special educator is already deployed as a coteacher in regular classrooms or in some other capacity at another tier in the new continuum of placements and services? Will schools be capable of providing children with certified special needs the "appropriate education" promised in IDEA 2004?

A Special Education "Technology" of Assessment and Instruction

We support the use of a multi-tiered approach to provide evidence-based instruction as early as possible to accelerate all children's learning. We believe, however, that there are at least two features essential to RTI's success: fewer tiers and special education as the last tier. Many past and current reformers in special and general education have overlooked the fact that special education has an evidence-based "technology" of assessment and instruction that was developed over 20–30 years by researchers and practitioners. This special education technology depends on student progress monitoring, and is a test–teach–test approach that is data-based, inductive, and recursive. It requires special educators to be experimenters: To try instructional program A and measure student progress. If A doesn't work well enough, try program B or a combination of A and B and again examine student progress. If this doesn't work, try something else and continue to systematically collect student outcome data.

Unlike coteaching, this assessment/instructional approach has been studied and described in hundreds of papers published in scholarly journals around the world. And unlike coteaching, which often casts special educators in the role of helper or aide (cf. Scruggs et al., 2007), this approach requires special educators to understand assessment and instruction; to become the most expert instructors in the school, the professional to whom the most difficult-to-teach students are sent. In the remainder of this chapter, we describe what special education would look like as a final tier to show how it can indeed be special. Toward this end, we follow a hypothetical student, Libby, who struggles in reading to illustrate how student progress monitoring data are used through the RTI tiers; to eventually identify her as LD; and to develop measurable annual goals, determine the adequacy of her progress toward meeting the goals, and formatively develop effective individualized instruction for her.

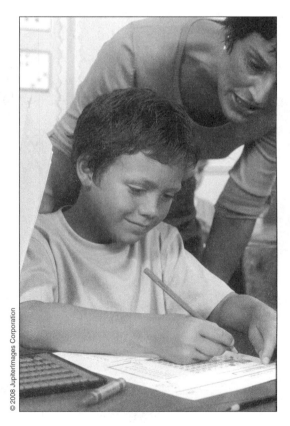
© 2008 JupiterImages Corporation

RTI at Lincoln Elementary School

Monitoring Early Reading Performance

Libby transferred to a new school district two months after starting first grade. At her new school, two alternate forms of word identification fluency (i.e., number of words read correctly per minute from a list of high-frequency, primary-level words) are given to every first grader during the third week of school. The student's average score is compared to normative data or to criterion scores to identify any student likely to be at risk for developing reading difficulties. Word identification fluency functions similarly to oral reading fluency (i.e., number of words read correctly per minute in connected text), which has been used with success for decades as a part of CBM (Deno, 1985) procedures for monitoring overall growth toward year-end reading goals in the elementary years. CBM is a research-validated form of progress monitoring and has contributed to improved student achievement when teachers use the data for instructional decision making (for review, see Fuchs & Fuchs, 1986; Stecker, Fuchs, & Fuchs, 2005; see also Chapter 2, this volume, for more information on CBM). Because many students score very low on oral reading fluency at the beginning of first grade (i.e., experience floor effects), word identification fluency is used at Lincoln Elementary to monitor reading growth across the entire first grade. Word identification fluency demonstrates sound technical characteristics for progress monitoring with good predictive and concurrent validity with end-of-year achievement tests (Fuchs, Fuchs, & Compton, 2004).

Ms. Montoya, Libby's first-grade teacher, administered to Libby two word identification fluency measures two weeks after she entered Lincoln Elementary (i.e., Week 9 in the school year). At five words read correctly in one minute, Libby scored markedly lower than her peers—even lower than peers' average score at the beginning of the school year. Ms. Montoya sent Libby's scores to her parents. She was concerned about Libby's performance, but she also didn't know anything about her first-grade instruction in her previous school and recognized that she may improve rapidly given well-designed teacher-directed instruction. Ms. Montoya included a note of concern about Libby's reading performance in the information sent home, but she also described how she would continue to monitor her growth in reading over the next two months.

Tier 1 Prevention: Ms. Montoya

Ms. Montoya used the district's code-based core reading program. Oral activities supported vocabulary and comprehension development. Ms. Montoya posted a description of class activities each week on her school's class webpage. She monitored Libby's progress weekly for the next two months on word identification fluency and sent home a copy of her progress monitoring chart every two weeks.

After eight weeks of progress monitoring, Ms. Montoya met with the school's Student Support Team to discuss Libby's lack of progress. The first phase (or first panel) in Figure 4.1 shows progress monitoring data for word identification fluency during Tier 1 instruction (i.e., instruction in the general education classroom). Libby's scores grew minimally from about 5 to 9 words read correctly per minute, or about .5 words per week growth on average. She fell significantly behind her peers who generally responded well to classroom instruction. Ms. Montoya checked all her students' scores on word identification fluency measures every few weeks, and the class currently ranged from 10 to 40 words read correctly in one minute with a class average of 28 words read correctly. Given Libby's weak performance level and minimal growth, the Student Support Team recommended that she enter Tier 2 supplemental instruction. Ms. Montoya contacted Libby's parents to explain this

FIGURE 4.1

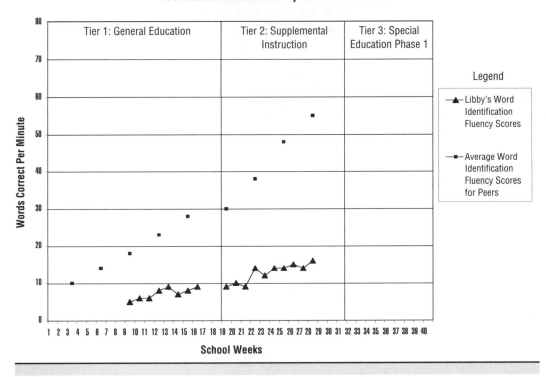

Word Identification Fluency Scores for Grade 1

recommendation and invited them to attend a conference to discuss this next step.

Tier 2 Prevention: Ms. McKnight

After returning from winter break, Libby entered Tier 2 with four other children. Ms. McKnight, a reading specialist, served as the intervention teacher and provided 30 minutes of Tier 2 instruction four days per week in phonemic awareness and phonics activities according to a prescribed, carefully developed sequence for 10 weeks. Ms. McKnight spent time modeling tasks and providing many opportunities for students to practice skills that had just been demonstrated. Ms. McKnight continued to monitor Libby's weekly progress on the word identification fluency task. Every 3–4 weeks during Tier 2 prevention, Ms. McKnight also checked her students' oral reading fluency on first-grade passages, because first graders typically read connected text as a part of daily instruction at this point in the year. She wanted to see whether her instructional strategies were helping students to generalize their skills to text reading.

Both Libby's level of performance and rate of improvement were less than anticipated across the 10 weeks of Tier 2 instruction. On word identification fluency, Libby read very slowly with scores of only 16 words read correctly per minute and a growth rate of about .7 words correct per week by the end of the instructional phase. Even with this very modest improvement, her word identification fluency scores fell significantly below her typical classmates' scores of about 55 words read correctly per minute and a weekly growth rate of almost 2.5 words correct. Her teachers reported that Libby could say sounds for about two thirds of the consonants but had difficulty blending sounds to read words. She also had a limited sight word vocabulary. However, she seemed to comprehend information adequately while listening to stories read aloud or during group discussion. When given first-grade passages, Libby was able to read only about 14 words correctly per minute in connected text. This poor performance caused concern and prompted Libby's teachers to consider her for Tier 3 intervention. The Student Support Team reviewed Libby's data and referred her for a possible learning disability. The second phase in Figure 4.1 depicts the progress monitoring data collected during Tier 2 instruction.

Because Libby's parents had been informed of their daughter's progress during first grade, they were not surprised when the school recommended more intensive instruction for her and an evaluation for a possible learning disability. With parental consent, a modified comprehensive evaluation was conducted across the next several weeks. Validated assessments and rating scales were administered to rule out possible vision and hearing problems, intellectual disability, and emotional/behavioral disability. Likewise, formal and informal tests helped educators eliminate speech/language disability and cultural and linguistic characteristics as possibly contributing to Libby's learning problems. Performance information from Libby's teachers and the progress monitoring data demonstrated continued nonresponsiveness to generally effective reading instruction and provided a large part of Libby's achievement data during the comprehensive evaluation. The multidisciplinary team, including Libby's parents, determined that Libby had a learning disability in basic reading skills and was in need of specialized services. The IEP team met to develop a long-range plan for individualized instruction. Consequently, special education services were delivered as Tier 3 intervention.

Tier 3 Intervention: Mr. Case

IEP GOAL DEVELOPMENT. The IEP team—which included Mr. Case, the school's special education teacher—needed to develop a measurable annual reading goal for Libby. This goal should always reflect overall reading achievement in a year's time. Consequently, the annual goal was set for the spring of Libby's second-grade year. Although her progress had been charted across the first-grade year with word identification fluency, oral reading fluency was considered a more robust measure of overall reading achievement because it requires multiple reading skills. The team also knew that it is a technically sound measure (Deno, 1985; Fuchs, Fuchs, Hosp, & Jenkins, 2001). On these bases, the team chose to use it for developing Libby's IEP goal. Although the team already had data on Libby's oral reading fluency for first-grade measures (i.e., about 14 words correct per minute), they gathered baseline data on second-grade passages as well. Libby's average score on two second-grade passages was 12 words read correctly per minute, which approximated her average score of 14 on the first-grade passages. Libby seemed to read similar words across all the passages. Because her performance was comparable in both first- and second-grade texts, and she would be a second grader the following year, the team decided to select second-grade text for establishing the long-range goal.

Mr. Case, the special education teacher, thought the gap between Libby's performance and her peers' could be closed with intensive, specialized instruction. The IEP team set 84 words read correctly per minute in second-grade passages as Libby's annual goal to be achieved by spring of her second-grade year (i.e., one year from initiating special education services). The team considered several factors in setting this long-range goal. First, it examined how well students typically read by the end of second grade. A number of progress monitoring systems publish benchmarks, or minimum scores, by grade level at various points in the school year for judging continued reading success. The IEP team consulted Hasbrouck and Tindal's (2006) published norms for oral reading fluency that included a sample of more than 20,000 second graders, including special needs children and English-language learners. In spring, this normative sample scored an average 89 words read correctly per minute at the 50th percentile; 61 words at the 25th percentile.

Second, the team looked at "average" and "ambitious" rates of growth for second graders (see Fuchs, Fuchs, Hamlett, Walz, & Germann, 1993). Average and ambitious rates of growth per week were an additional 1.5 and 2.0 words read correctly, respectively. Weekly growth rate could be multiplied by the total number of instructional weeks left to meet to the annual goal and that number, in turn, could be added to the student's beginning

© 2008 JupiterImages Corporation

performance to determine an average, or reasonable, goal. There were 36 instructional weeks (i.e., 8 weeks left in first grade, 28 weeks in second grade) before the date of Libby's annual goal. The IEP team decided that they needed to accelerate Libby's growth and deliberately calculated an ambitious (not average) growth rate of 2 additional words read correctly per week. They multiplied the 2 words per week by 36 instructional weeks to yield 72 words, which they added to Libby's baseline performance of 12 words to produce the annual goal of 84 words read correctly per minute. The IEP team compared this ambitious goal (for Libby) to normative data for spring of second grade and determined that Libby's goal fell within an average range. Her parents wanted her to be able to read like her peers and supported the provision of intensive services. Her IEP statement for current level of performance was, "Given passages written at the second-grade level, Libby currently reads aloud 12 words correctly in 1 minute." Her annual goal was, "Given passages written at the second-grade level, Libby will read aloud and correctly at least 84 words per minute following 36 instructional weeks."

DATA–BASED INSTRUCTIONAL DECISION MAKING. The graph in Figure 4.2 shows Libby's IEP progress monitoring data. The dark triangle in the first panel of the figure represents her baseline performance at Week 32 of her *first-grade* year on oral reading fluency in second-grade passages. The open triangle in the last panel of the figure depicts the long-term goal set for Week 32 (instructional Week 28) of Libby's *second-grade* year. The line connecting baseline performance in first grade and the annual goal in second grade is the "goal line," which depicts the rate at which she needs to progress through the curriculum for the remainder of first grade and in second grade. Libby's teachers continued to monitor her progress frequently, and after every 8 data points, compared her rate of improvement against the goal line to judge whether she was making adequate progress. When her growth rate was less steep than anticipated (i.e., as compared with the goal line), her special education teacher, Mr. Case,

FIGURE 4.2

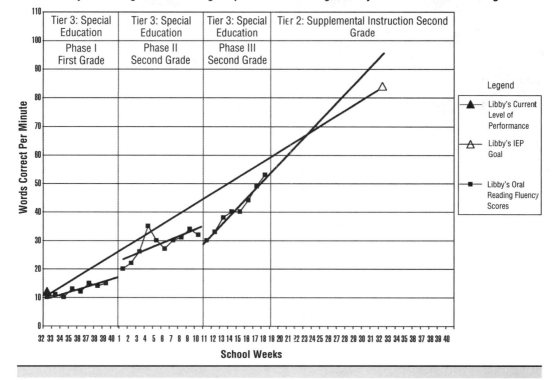

Libby's IEP Progress Monitoring Graph for Oral Reading Fluency on Second-Grade Passages

modified instruction to stimulate better achievement. (See the "lines of best fit" in the first three panels of the figure.) When Libby made better-than-anticipated progress (see the third panel), the team raised her goal and considered whether a trial of less intensive instruction, such as that provided in Tier 2, was warranted. Thus, progress monitoring data were used within an RTI model as an objective basis for determining when modifications were necessary within instructional tiers and when movement in and out of instructional tiers appeared appropriate.

INSTRUCTIONAL IMPLEMENTATION. Mr. Case worked with Libby, and two other students with similar instructional needs for 75 minutes

© 2008 JupiterImages Corporation

daily on literacy activities specific to Libby's needs. This instruction supplemented, rather than substituted for, her core reading program. Because of her weak word identification skills, Mr. Case focused heavily on decoding skills, including practice on letter–sound correspondences for consonants and short vowels, blending activities to sound out words, and timed drills with high-frequency sight words. Mr. Case also developed word lists and short reading passages that incorporated the decodable patterns and sight words that Libby had been practicing. Although some oral activities supported vocabulary development and comprehension instruction, Mr. Case spent the greatest proportion of time helping Libby to read words and connected text independently. Mr. Case primarily used first-grade materials for instruction; however, he continued to assess Libby's oral reading fluency on second-grade passages. The trend line, or slope, through the last eight weeks of instruction in first grade (see the first panel in Figure 4.2) illustrates Libby's increasing progress, but it fell considerably below the desired rate when compared to her annual goal line.

Libby started second grade in August and continued to receive both core reading instruction in her general education classroom and special education with Mr. Case. Mr. Case spent two weeks in intensive review of previously learned skills before adding additional sight words, teaching sound correspondence for common letter combinations, and introducing decodable books for reading practice for the next 8 weeks. He also directed Libby to spell and write the words she was reading. During these first 10 weeks of school, Mr. Case collected weekly progress monitoring data. Afterward, he calculated Libby's rate of progress: Although she had one score that exceeded her goal line, the overall trend of her performance was less steep. (See especially the second panel of Figure 4.2 and the superimposed trend line and goal line.)

Consequently, Mr. Case wanted to improve Libby's rate of growth once again. He considered her performance and aspects of his instructional program that could be modified to better meet her reading needs. Because she was improving, but not improving at the necessary rate, Mr. Case continued with his decoding instruction. However, he added fluency-building activities and expanded Libby's repertoire of reading selections. He also began to use second-grade instructional material. He included the rereading of stories used earlier in the year in Libby's core program and he previewed with her the vocabulary and specific skills for upcoming lessons in her general education classroom.

In this way, Mr. Case relied on progress monitoring data to determine the relative effectiveness of his instructional program. Periodically, he compared the rate of his students' progress against the anticipated and necessary rate of progress (i.e., the goal line) to judge how well his instruction was working. Over time, he was able to develop more effective instruction for her by introducing program modifications that better suited her unique learning needs.

MOVEMENT AMONG TIERS. As evidenced in Figure 4.2, Libby made substantial progress during Tier 3, or special education. Libby's trend of performance during this tier of instruction actually exceeded the anticipated and necessary rate of growth illustrated by the goal line in Figure 4.2. If Libby's progress continued in this fashion, her performance likely would exceed her annual IEP goal. Mr. Case made this point when he met with the IEP team. The team decided that Libby's goal should be raised to 95 words read correctly per minute and that one cycle of Tier 2 instruction should be conducted without Tier 3 intensive intervention. Mr. Case would continue to collect progress monitoring data and to consult with Libby's teachers. If she were to continue to progress well, she would remain in Tier 2 instruction to the end of the school year. If the data showed a slowing of progress, Tier 3 instruction would be reinstituted.

Thus, the IEP team did not release Libby fully from special education. Her placement changed to Tier 2 services, and this supplemental instruction time was reduced to 30 minutes per day, five days per week. However, Mr. Case continued to monitor her progress toward her IEP goal and to consult with the Tier 2 reading specialist.

In this scenario, progress monitoring data were used to direct the level of intensity of instructional support she needed. These data were used both to monitor Libby's responsiveness to instruction and to judge the overall effectiveness of the instructional program. Her movement in and out of instructional tiers was flexible, with special and general education services working in coordinated fashion. Once she demonstrated a desirable growth trajectory without intensive special education provided in Tier 3, the IEP team could dismiss her entirely from special education services.

RTI's Promise and Challenges

RTI has important potential advantages. Reconfiguring general education and special education into a system of multiple layers of increasingly intensive, evidence-based instruction should make it more responsive to students at risk for school failure and better able to address the learning needs of a diverse student body. Moreover, with two or more instructional tiers in general education, academically at-risk students may get more quickly the instruction they require without waiting months or years to qualify for special education. And with more at-risk children appropriately served in general education's various instructional tiers, there should be fewer "false positives" (i.e., students who appear disabled but are not) who enter special education, thus making the disability-identification process more accurate and valid.

Student progress monitoring (i.e., CBM) plays a central role in RTI. In early fall of the school year, it helps classroom teachers identify students who may be at risk for academic failure. Teachers use CBM to monitor the students' progress—or their responsiveness to instruction—for five to eight weeks and those deemed at risk then participate in the more intensive instruction at the second tier, where other educators also monitor the students' progress. The progress monitoring at Tier 2 helps instructors distinguish between responders and nonresponders; those seen as nonresponsive are evaluated for special education. In special education, CBM is used to develop measurable and ambitious annual goals, to monitor progress toward those goals, and to formatively develop effective individualized instruction. We hope we have adequately illustrated how and why progress monitoring is so important to any RTI approach.

Despite the promises associated with RTI, and despite the educational community having useful knowledge about how to implement it, major issues remain. Among the most important is whether practitioners will indeed implement evidence-based instruction and assessment practices with fidelity. Practitioners, including school administrators, must find the resources necessary to support high-quality instruction at all levels of practice. This will require ongoing professional development and schoolwide organization and commitment. Without this, RTI will fail as both early intervention and as a more valid method of disability identification. Also, progress monitoring measures must be technically sound, and research evidence should guide use of these data for decision making. Not all progress monitoring measures are equal. Few are valid for all educational purposes. Some are better at helping educators make decision X; others decision Y.

© 2008 JupiterImages Corporation

Practitioners should make use of resources such as the information on the website of the National Center on Student Progress Monitoring (www.studentprogress.org) to inform themselves about how best to proceed.

Additionally, technical questions relate to the number of tiers that should be included in an RTI model, the length and number of preventive treatment phases within each tier, the frequency of progress monitoring (e.g., once or twice per week), and the comprehensiveness of special education evaluation. (For discussions of these and other issues, see Fuchs, Mock, Morgan, & Young, 2003; Fuchs & Fuchs, 2006; Fuchs & Young, 2006; Gerber, 2003; Mastropieri & Scruggs, 2005.)

What Role for Special Education?

Yet another important question is, What role should special education play in an RTI framework? There are those with a dark view of special education: hasn't worked, isn't working, won't ever be effective. These critics offer two visions of special education in the context of RTI. Both call for a "blurring" (see McLaughlin, 2006) of general and special education, a polite way of saying that we lose nothing from desired practice if its identity is weakened beyond recognition. One group seems to think that with a large enough number of general education tiers there will be no need for special education. Put differently, promoters of this view recognize the real-world importance of our fictitious Mr. Case—or more precisely the importance of the kind of individualized, data-based, and recursive education he provides. But they want this most intensive instruction to be implemented in general education and by general educators, presumably because they do not trust that it can happen in special education.

The second group, in which we include McLaughlin (2006), NASDSE/CASE (2006), and others, folds much of special education (all of special education for the so-called children with high-incidence disabilities) into general education tiers. In a sense, this is the more troubling approach because, as expressed by McLaughlin and others, special education becomes a mere appendage of general education instruction—a supplement to it. In accordance with this vision, special educators help general educators tweak their instruction—modify it, extend it, elaborate on it. Currently, the most frequently offered example of this arrangement is coteaching despite that there is virtually no scientific evidence that it has anything to do with individualized, data-based, recursive, systematic instruction. We predict that should special education be redefined in terms of practices like coteaching, many students with special needs will not get the appropriate education that is their legal right and they will experience a lifetime of diminished opportunity.

In sum, one group preserves at least the idea of individualized, data-based, recursive instruction, but would take it from special education and expect general education to implement it. The second group would transform special education instruction and special educators' instructional roles in the misguided belief that individualized instruction is unnecessary if not counterproductive because, it is alleged, it leads to a lack of accountability.

So, What's to Be Done?

If RTI is properly conducted it will lead to the identification of an unknown number of nonresponders (hopefully far fewer than today but surely more than predicted by McLaughlin, 2006), irrespective of the number of tiers, choice of instructional programs and curricula, amount and quality of professional development, and so forth. What will be done with these most-difficult-to-teach students? We believe that they should get the kind of instruction Mr. Case provided Libby. Coteaching, cooperative learning, and other so-called inclusion strategies like "accommodating the curriculum," are not instructional substitutes for these students. Anyone suggesting otherwise simply does not understand the students or the instruction we have described, or the research that supports its use. Moreover, the Mr. Cases of the education world are more likely than Ms. McKnight and Ms. Montoya to provide this expert instruction because they are more likely to have been trained by (an admittedly small number of) special education academics who have researched this instruction, written textbooks describing it, established training programs based on it, and come from a pedagogic tradition that values individual differences and looks at academically vulnerable students as "their" children. Few general educators can claim such a tradition or preference.

We support RTI because we see it as a means of reforming general education, making it more responsive to at-risk students. We support it also because we hope it forces a reconceptualization and reconfiguration of special education, making it more effective with children with disabilities. If general education is redefined in terms of multiple tiers of increasingly intensive, evidence-based instruction, it prompts the question, What's special about special education in this framework? The answer is that special education must be the most intensive tier at which, by definition, instruction is data-based, individualized, and recursive.

AUTHOR NOTE
We thank Margaret McLaughlin for helping us access her paper on standards-driven reform. Thanks, too, to Tom Scruggs, Margo Mastropieri, Naomi Zigmond, and Lee Swanson for sending us their work on coteaching. Finally, we thank Dan Hallahan for his thoughtful comments on an earlier draft. None of these colleagues necessarily shares the ideas or positions expressed in this chapter.

REFERENCES
Baker, J.M., & Zigmond, N. (1990). Are regular classes equipped to accommodate students with learning disabilities? *Exceptional Children*, *56*(6), 515–526.

Batsche, G., Elliott, J., Graden, J.L., Grimes, J., Kovaleski, J.F., Prasse, D., et al. (2005). *Response to intervention: Policy considerations and implementation.* Alexandria, VA: National Association of State Directors of Special Education.

Carnine, D.W., Silbert, J., Kame'enui, E.J., & Tarver, S.G. (2004). *Direct instruction reading* (4th ed.). Upper Saddle River, NJ: Prentice Hall.

Compton, D.L., Fuchs, D., Fuchs, L.S., & Bryant, J.D. (2006). Selecting at-risk readers in first grade for early intervention: A two-year longitudinal study of decision rules and procedures. *Journal of Educational Psychology, 98*(2), 394–409.

De La Paz, S., Owen, B., Harris, K., & Graham, S. (2000). Riding Elvis's motorcycle: Using self-regulated strategy development to PLAN and WRITE for a state writing exam. *Learning Disabilities Research & Practice, 15*(2), 101–109.

Delquadri, J.C., Greenwood, C.R., Whorton, D., Carta, J.J., & Hall, R.V. (1986). Classwide peer tutoring. *Exceptional Children, 52*(6), 535–542.

Deno, E. (1970). Special education as developmental capital. *Exceptional Children, 37*(3), 229–237.

Deno, S.L. (1985). Curriculum-based measurement: The emerging alternative. *Exceptional Children, 52*(3), 219–232.

Deshler, D.D., Schumaker, J.B., Lenz, B.K., Bulgren, J.A., Hock, M.F., Knight, J., et al. (2001). Ensuring content-area learning by secondary students with learning disabilities. *Learning Disabilities Research & Practice, 16*(2), 96–108.

Elliott, J. (2007, April 18). *Response-to-intervention.* National Center for Learning Disabilities LD talk. Retrieved February 9, 2007, from www.ncld.org/content/view/930

Fuchs, D., & Deshler, D.D. (2007). What we need to know about responsiveness to intervention (and shouldn't be afraid to ask). *Learning Disabilities Research & Practice, 22*(2), 129–136.

Fuchs, D., & Fuchs, L.S. (2005). Peer-assisted learning strategies: Promoting word recognition, fluency, and reading comprehension in young children. *Journal of Special Education, 39*(1), 34–44.

Fuchs, D., Fuchs, L.S., & Compton, D.L. (2004). Identifying reading disability by responsiveness-to-instruction: Specifying measures and criteria. *Learning Disability Quarterly, 27*(4), 216–227.

Fuchs, D., Mock, D., Morgan, P., & Young, C.L. (2003). Responsiveness-to-intervention: Definitions, evidence, and implications for the learning disabilities construct. *Learning Disabilities Research and Practice, 18*(3), 157–171.

Fuchs, D., & Young, C.L. (2006). On the irrelevance of intelligence in predicting responsiveness to reading instruction. *Exceptional Children, 73*(1), 8–30.

Fuchs, L.S., & Fuchs, D. (1986). Effects of systematic formative evaluation: A meta-analysis. *Exceptional Children, 53*(3), 199–208.

Fuchs, L.S., & Fuchs, D. (2006). Identifying learning disabilities with RTI. *Perspectives, 32*(1), 39–43.

Fuchs, L.S., Fuchs, D., & Compton, D.L. (2004). Monitoring early reading development in first grade: Word identification fluency versus nonsense word fluency. *Exceptional Children, 71*(7), 7–21.

Fuchs, L.S., Fuchs, D., Hamlett, C.L., Walz, L., & Germann, G. (1993). Formative evaluation of academic progress: How much growth can we expect? *School Psychology Review, 22*(1), 27–48.

Fuchs, L.S., Fuchs, D., Hosp, M.K., & Jenkins, J.R. (2001). Oral reading fluency as an indicator of reading competence: A theoretical, empirical, and historical analysis. *Scientific Studies of Reading, 5*(3), 239–256.

Gartner, A., & Lipsky, D. (1987). Beyond special education: Toward a quality system for all students. *Harvard Educational Review, 57*(4), 367–395.

Gerber, M.M. (2003, December). *Teachers are still the test: Limitations to response to instruction strategies for identifying children with learning disabilities.* Paper presented at the National Research Center on Learning Disabilities symposium, Kansas City.

Greenwood, C.R., Delquadri, J.C., & Hall, R.V. (1989). Longitudinal effects of classwide peer tutoring. *Journal of Educational Psychology, 81*(3), 371–383.

Grimes, J. (2002). *Responsiveness to interventions: The next step in special education identification, service and exiting decision making.* Revision of paper written for the Office of Special Education Programs, US Department of Education, and presented at OSEP's LD Summit conference, Washington, DC.

Hall, R.V., Delquadri, J.C., Greenwood, C.R., & Thurston, L. (1982). The importance of opportunity to respond in children's academic success. In E. Edgar, N. Haring, J. Jenkins, & C. Pious (Eds.), *Mentally handicapped children: Education and training* (pp. 107–140). Baltimore: University Park Press.

Hardman, M. (2007, March 29). *Redesigning the preparation of general and special education teachers: Collaboration within a school-wide system of support.* Testimony before the Committee on Education and Labor subcommittee on early childhood, elementary and secondary education, US House of Representatives.

Hasbrouck, J., & Tindal, G.A. (2006). Oral reading fluency norms: A valuable assessment tool for reading teachers. *The Reading Teacher, 59*(7), 636–644.

Ikeda, M.J., & Gustafson, J.K. (2002). *Heartland AEA 11's problem solving process: Impact on issues related to special education* (Research Report No. 2002-01). Johnston, IA: Heartland Area Education Agency 11.

Johnson, D.W., & Johnson, R.T. (1994). *Learning together and alone: Cooperative, competitive, and individualistic learning.* Boston: Allyn & Bacon.

Lesgold, A.M., & Resnick, L. (1982). How reading difficulties develop: Perspectives from a longitudinal study. In J. Das, R. Mulcahy, & A. Wall (Eds.), *Theory and research in learning disabilities* (pp. 155–187). New York: Plenum.

Lyon, G.R., Fletcher, J.M., Shaywitz, S.E., Shaywitz, B.A., Torgesen, J.K., Wood, F.B., et al. (2001). Rethinking learning disabilities. In C.E. Finn, Jr., A.J. Rotherham, & C.R. Hokanson, Jr. (Eds.), *Rethinking special education for a new century* (pp. 259–287). Washington, DC: Thomas B. Fordham Foundation and Progressive Policy Institute

Mastropieri, M.A., & Scruggs, T.E. (2005). Feasibility and consequences of response to intervention: Examination of the issues and scientific evidence as a model for the identification of individuals with learning disabilities. *Journal of Learning Disabilities, 38*(6), 525–531.

McDermott, R.P., & Aron, J. (1978). Pirandello in the classroom: On the possibility of equal educational opportunity in American culture. In M.C. Reynolds (Ed.), *Futures of education for exceptional students* (pp. 41–64). Reston, VA: Council for Exceptional Children.

McIntosh, R., Vaughn, S., Schumm, J.S., & Haager, D., Lee, O. (1994). Observations of students with learning disabilities in general education classrooms. *Exceptional Children, 60*(3), 249–261.

McLaughlin, M.J. (2006). *Closing the achievement gap and students with disabilities: The new meaning of a "free and appropriate public education."* Unpublished manuscript.

McMaster, K.L.N., Fuchs, D., Fuchs, L.S., & Comptor, D.L. (2005). Responding to nonresponders: An experimental field trial of identification and intervention methods. *Exceptional Children, 71*(4), 445–463.

McMaster, K.L.N., & Fuchs, D. (2002). Effects of cooperative learning on the academic achievement of students with learning disabilities: An update of Tateyama-Sniezek's review. *Learning Disabilities: Research & Practice, 17*(2), 107–117.

Minneapolis Public Schools. (2001). *Problem solving model: Introduction for all staff.* Minneapolis, MN: Author.

Murawski, W.W., & Swanson, L.H. (2001). A meta-analysis of co-teaching research: Where are the data? *Remedial and Special Education, 22*(5), 258–267.

National Association of State Directors of Special Education/Council of Administrators of Special Education. (2006, May). *Response to intervention: A joint paper by the National Association of State Directors of Special Education and the Council of Administrators of Special Education.* Alexandria, VA: Author.

National Center for Education Statistics. (2005, April). *Common core of data: Table 52.* Washington, DC: Author.

No Child Left Behind Act of 2001, Pub. L. No. 107-110, 115 Stat. 1425 (2002).

O'Sullivan, P.J., Ysseldyke, J.E., Christenson, S.L., & Thurlow, M.L. (1990). Mildly handicapped elementary students' opportunity to learn during reading instruction in mainstream and special education settings. *Reading Research Quarterly, 25*(2), 131–146.

Pearpoint, J., & Forest, M. (1992). Foreword. In S. Stainback & W. Stainback (Eds.), *Curriculum considerations in inclusive classrooms: Facilitating learning for all students* (pp. xv–xviii). Baltimore: Brookes.

Reynolds, M.C. (1962). A framework for considering some issues in special education. *Exceptional Children, 28*(7), 367–370.

Schemo, D.J., & Medina, J. (2007, October 27). Disabled pupils, private schools, public money. *The New York Times,* p. 1, 14.

Scruggs, T.E., Mastropieri, M.A., & McDuffie, K.A. (2007). Co-teaching in inclusive classrooms: A meta-synthesis of qualitative research. *Exceptional Children, 73*(4), 392–416.

Slavin, R.E., & Madden, N.A. (2000). Research on achievement outcomes of success for all: A summary and response to critics. *Phi Delta Kappan, 82*(1), 38–40, 59–66.

Slavin, R.E., & Madden, N.A. (2003). *Success for All/Roots & Wings: Summary of research on achievement outcomes*. Baltimore: Center for Research on the Education of Students Placed At Risk.

Stainback, S., & Stainback, W. (1992). *Curriculum considerations in inclusive classrooms: Facilitating learning for all students*. Baltimore: Paul Brookes.

Stecker, P.M., Fuchs, L.S., & Fuchs, D. (2005). Using curriculum-based measurement to improve student achievement: Review of research. *Psychology in the Schools, 42*(8), 795–819.

Taylor, S.J. (1988). Caught in the continuum: A critical analysis of the principle of least restrictive environment. *Journal of the Association for Persons With Severe Handicaps, 13*(1), 41–53.

Thousand, J.S., & Villa, R.A. (1990). Strategies for educating learners with severe disabilities within their local home schools and communities. *Focus on Exceptional Children, 23*(3), 1–24.

Tomsho, R. (2007, August 16). Is an early-help program shortchanging kids? *The Wall Street Journal*, p. B1.

Torgesen, J.K. (2000). Individual differences in response to early interventions in reading: The lingering problem of treatment resisters. *Learning Disabilities: Research & Practice, 15*(1), 55–64.

Vellutino, F.R., Scanlon, D.M., Sipay, E.R., Small, S.G., Pratt, A., Chen, R., et al. (1996). Cognitive profiles of difficult-to-remediate and readily remediated poor readers: Early intervention as a vehicle for distinguishing between cognitive and experiential deficits as basic causes of specific reading disability. *Journal of Educational Psychology, 88*(4), 601–638.

Walsh, M. (2007, October 17). Court is split on IDEA private-placement case. *Education Week*, p. 18, 22.

Zigmond, N. (2006). Reading and writing in co-taught secondary school social studies classrooms: A reality check. *Reading & Writing Quarterly, 22*(3), 249–268.

Zigmond, N., & Baker, J.M. (1994). Is the mainstream a more appropriate educational setting for Randy? A case study of one student with learning disabilities. *Learning Disabilities: Research & Practice, 9*(2), 108–117.

Zigmond, N., & Matta, D. (2005). Value added of the special education teacher in secondary school co-taught classes. In T.E. Scruggs & M.A. Mastropieri (Eds.), *Advances in learning and behavioral disabilities: Vol. 17. Research in secondary schools* (pp. 55–76). Oxford, UK: Elsevier.

Implications of RTI for the Reading Teacher

Timothy Shanahan

while back I was making a presentation of a literacy teaching framework that I use in my work. After most of a day–long seminar, one principal looked at me sideways and said, "It isn't your framework."

"What do you mean?"

"The reason the kids read better. It isn't your framework," she repeated.

"What is it then?"

"You're just aggressive about kids' learning."

No one has ever said anything nicer about me. And that is how I feel about Response to Intervention (RTI). RTI is not a specific program and you can't buy it from a publisher. But RTI is valuable because it is a particularly effective institutional way to be aggressive about kids' learning.

No instructional method, approach, technique, strategy, or scheme has ever been found to be 100% effective. Even in the most advantaged and highest achieving school districts some students struggle; and of course, in less advantaged schools, there are many more students who have difficulty mastering what it takes to be a reader.

Response to Intervention: A Framework for Reading Educators edited by Douglas Fuchs, Lynn S. Fuchs, and Sharon Vaughn. Copyright 2008 by the International Reading Association.

Sadly, despite the universality of the problem, schools often have not been especially energetic in their attempts to make sure that all students succeed. In the worst cases, classroom instruction can be dismal and the opportunity to get any extra help totally absent. Far more frequently, quality classroom instruction is not impossible, just hit-or-miss, and there is often some kind of additional help provided, perhaps in the form of a Title I reading class or a special education class. The research evidence on such programmatic efforts is mixed at best, suggesting that they help under some circumstances, but not under many others (Aaron, 1997; Allington, 1994; Jarvis-Janik, 1993; Swanson & Hoskyn, 1998). In some cases, these programmatic supports are simply ineffective, while other times the quality is OK, but the amount of help provided is insufficient.

RTI seems like a better solution than that usually somewhat haphazard pastiche of supports. RTI tries to make sure that classroom teaching is "up to snuff" and that when a student does falter, there will be a rich, and ultimately, sufficient instructional response to his or her reading needs.

What Counts as RTI?

Because RTI is not actually a program, there are lots of variants in what counts as RTI (National Association of State Directors of Special Education [NASDSE], 2005). There are three-tiered RTI models and four-tiered models, and even with those models not everyone agrees as to what the different tiers may refer to. So what is common to all RTI approaches? Most educators seem to accept that the first tier of response is provided to all students in the form of high-quality classroom teaching, and the final tier means moving the student into a highly targeted and supportive special education program—but the number and type of interventions and supports in the middle varies greatly. The middle tier(s) may include extra instruction within the classroom by the regular classroom teacher, or there may be extra help from a different teacher beyond what can be provided in the classroom, and such help might be given even beyond the school day or the school year. Let it suffice that in RTI there is classroom instruction for all, a rich and varied menu of additional help in the middle for those who struggle, and special education of some form for those who do not respond adequately to the additional help (hence "response to intervention" is the gatekeeper to special education, because if the student is learning adequately from the improvements that are provided there is presumably no need for a special education placement).

Another point held in common among various RTI conceptions is the use of student assessment data to make decisions, and that there will be planning on the basis of this evidence to provide the best and most appropriate response to the students' needs (NASDSE, 2005). The successful use of RTI requires the involvement of a team of professional educators who, together, try to meet every student's needs. Neither teachers nor students can be isolated in RTI because the increasing intensification of these efforts requires the coordination of the skills and involvement of a variety of professionals, including reading professionals.

> **The successful use of RTI requires the involvement of a team of professional educators who, together, try to meet every student's needs.**

The purpose of this chapter is to consider the role of the reading teacher in successful RTI programs. First, I will explore the varied roles that reading professionals take within schools and then will consider what reading teachers have to offer to help make RTI an effective instructional response to students' learning needs.

The Nature of Reading Professionals

There are many kinds of reading professionals: reading teachers, remedial reading teachers, reading specialists, literacy coaches, reading resource specialists, and so on (Bean, 2003; Dole, Liang,

Watkins, & Wiggins, 2006). Districts and states differ in how and if they use these designations and so the approach taken here is to be inclusive—any reading professionals whose duties range beyond the scope of the regular classroom teacher (classroom reading teachers are critical as well, but their role is already addressed in Chapter 4). This consideration of the potential contributions of reading professionals in RTI is not limited to any particular job category or title, as reading teachers can play an important role within RTI efforts regardless of their actual job titles. If there is any doubt whether a particular job category falls within the scope of this chapter, I would assume that it does.

Districts and states differ not only in how reading professionals are referred to, but they also have varied requirements for the preparation of these teachers (Bean, 2003; Dole et al., 2006). Reading teachers should be included in RTI decision making and program implementation because of their specialized and deep knowledge in the teaching of reading. The whole idea of RTI is to improve and intensify the education provided to students who have trouble learning, and accordingly, the teachers who are helping guide the decisions for how to do this best must possess a great deal of knowledge about the teaching of reading—there would be no good reason for inviting them to the table otherwise. Unfortunately, some schools do manage to hire reading teachers or coaches without adequate or appropriate professional preparation. Although this chapter attempts to be inclusive of the varied titles used to designate reading professionals, it is not equally broadminded about the value of substantial preparation for these individuals. Knowledgeable reading teachers can play an important role in many aspects of RTI; those with a title and inadequate preparation cannot. The International Reading Association (IRA) has issued various documents on preparation standards for reading professionals of various types, and these can serve as a good starting point for ensuring that reading teachers have the knowledge and skills needed to successfully improve a school reading program (IRA, 2000a, 2000b, 2003, 2004).

Reading teachers should have a substantial understanding of the developmental continuum of learning to read. Such teachers should know how to support decoding and the phonological skills underlying decoding, as well as reading fluency, vocabulary, comprehension strategies, and the maintenance of reading  motivation. They should also have a firm grasp of sound assessment strategies and procedures, as well as an understanding of instructional texts and other materials that can support the successful teaching of reading. Typically, reading teachers have a special knowledge of the needs of struggling readers, and such teachers have often had extensive practicum experience and guidance in how to help such students to progress.

Reading professionals also vary in the functions they play within schools. This variation takes place along a continuum, from services for teachers and other professionals to the direct delivery of instruction to the students themselves (Bean, 2003). Those duties might include providing professional development for teachers, reading instruction for struggling learners, diagnosis and assessment services, and supervision for the school reading program. The purpose of this chapter is not to try to recommend what the best combination of services may be, but to recognize the diversity of roles often played by reading teachers. Because several of these roles or functions are specifically relevant to RTI, and if carried out well, would help schools to do a better job in teaching students to read, this chapter will explore a varied agenda of contributions that the reading teacher could make. I am not recommending that all reading teachers try to do all of these things, but many of the duties that are included in the reading teachers' job could be an important asset to a successful RTI effort.

Providing Professional Development

The idea of reading coaches or literacy coaches has certainly caught on (Dole et al., 2006). Increasing numbers of reading professionals are in jobs that focus wholly or largely on providing professional development to other teachers. The first order of business in making sure that students do well in learning to read is to make sure that classroom instruction is of reasonably high quality. High-quality classroom reading instruction has many dimensions, but none is more important than a well-prepared teacher.

In efforts to make certain that classroom teaching is good enough to succeed with most students, the reading coach can be extremely useful (Sykes, 1999). Coaches, by the nature of their duties, must spend a lot of time in other teachers' classrooms. This time is spent observing and giving feedback (coaching or mentoring) and doing demonstration lessons and the like.

Coaching efforts of this type can be general, of course, with the coach simply helping teachers to deliver a reading program. Over time, one would hope that such coaching would get more purposeful and data based. For instance, one possibility is for coaches to focus on making sure that teachers know how to teach all the key elements of reading (e.g., phonics, fluency, comprehension) or how to use a particular core program effectively. However, another possibility would be to look at the assessment data collected on students in the various classrooms. Looking at these data for the whole school or for particular grade levels can be informative. Are there particular patterns to the weaknesses? If the students in one class aren't doing very well with some aspect of literacy learning, but students in another class are, this might suggest the need for

© 2008 JupiterImages Corporation

more targeted support for that one teacher in whatever the gap may be. On the other hand, perhaps the assessment would reveal that students generally are doing better with some aspect of reading but not so well with another—that might suggest a schoolwide effort to improve teaching in the lagging area of concern.

Coaching is often focused on a teachers' overall instructional performance. This means that a coach working with a teacher on fluency might put the main emphasis on making certain that the teacher knew effective methods for teaching fluency, that he or she had appropriate materials, that enough fluency time was scheduled, and so on. That is a very appropriate way to mentor. However, in the context of RTI, the coach might take a very different approach. Perhaps the classroom teacher is providing reasonably high-quality fluency instruction and that only a handful of the students are struggling in this area. In that context, it is possible for the coach to provide a more targeted kind of assistance. Rather than trying to improve fluency instruction overall, perhaps the coach will observe the experiences of the students who are not doing well. That kind of focused observation might reveal specific weaknesses in how students are partnered for paired reading, or what the match of the student is to the text, or how much opportunity those students get to respond or participate within the lessons, or the amount or type of guidance provided to the students by the teacher. Changing these teaching behaviors can be hard work and a coach can help the teacher to work out an improvement plan and facilitate its implementation. This kind of support is not an instructional intervention, but it can be instrumental in improving the reading instruction provided to struggling readers.

Classroom teachers differ in how successful they are in delivering lessons. These differences can be evident from observing classroom practices alone. For instance, effective phonics lessons provide students with time to decode words or write from dictation—to actually practice the decoding and encoding. When visiting a classroom, a coach may recognize the lack of such elements within a lesson and would require no data beyond what was seen in order to help the teacher to do better. But what if the instruction seems to be good, but just isn't working for some students? That's where learning data comes in. Classrooms usually differ in the proportion of students who are succeeding with particular aspects of instruction. For example, an examination of the phonemic awareness data from several kindergarten classes after several weeks of teaching revealed that as few as 6 of 20 students were struggling in some classrooms, and as many as 18 of 20 in some others. Knowing these proportions would allow the coach to target his or her efforts, and they might lead to some guided observations by the less successful teachers in the more effective classrooms.

One of the hardest things for classroom teachers to do is to provide differentiated instruction for students. Such instruction might involve the teacher providing special lessons to certain students who are having difficulty learning. The lessons themselves may not pose any special challenge for the teacher—in fact, these could be the same lessons taught previously, but now with greater focus and intensity because of being offered in a small-group context as opposed to a classroom context.

The coach can also help out in the interpretation of data, both on a within-class and across-school basis. In order for RTI to work effectively, teachers have to be able to make sound decisions about student needs. Who is failing to learn adequately? With what are they having difficulty? What would be a sound and efficient response to the pattern of needs being displayed? The reading teacher can be a useful partner in interpreting such data and translating them into sound instructional practice.

In all of these examples, the reading specialist is enhancing RTI by improving the basic classroom instruction or the within-class intervention efforts of those classroom teachers. But the specialists can also have a positive impact on the special education programs as well. Special education teachers, because of the range of responsibilities they hold, are by necessity generalists. That means that the reading teacher will likely know more about reading curriculum and instruction per se and can make valuable professional development contributions to the teachers in the special education programs. The increasing attention to the professional development duties of reading teachers has resulted in the development of a rich collection of resource guides that can help reading teachers with this part of the work (Bean, 2003; Hasbrouck & Denton, 2005; Toll, 2004; Walpole & McKenna, 2004; Wepner, Strickland, & Feeley, 2002).

Providing Reading Interventions

One of the hallmarks of RTI is that instructional interventions are provided against which student learning can be evaluated. Reading teachers can be invaluable for their ability to provide high-quality instruction to children who are having difficulty learning to read. There are many examples in the research literature in which students are provided this kind of teaching to good effect (e.g., Blachman et al., 2004; Fisher & Blachowicz, 2005; Hatcher et al., 2006; Linan-Thompson & Hickman-Davis, 2002; Mathes et al., 2005; O'Connor & Simic, 2002; Shanahan & Barr, 1995; Vaughn, Linan-Thompson, & Hickman, 2003). Such instruction has been found to improve children's reading achievement, to reduce special education placements, and the effects of such efforts can be long lived.

> **Reading teachers can be invaluable for their ability to provide high-quality instruction to children who are having difficulty learning to read.**

Interventions can take many forms, and reading teachers can successfully contribute to a plethora of such efforts. For example, it was noted in the previous section that students can get additional help right in their own classroom. Such support could be provided by the classroom teacher, as in the example, but perhaps this would be impossible—either because of the extensiveness of the problems or the abilities of the classroom teacher. In any event, there is no

reason why the remedial work of the reading specialist has to be implemented outside of the classroom. So-called "push-in" programs, in which a reading teacher comes into the classroom to deliver instruction or support on a targeted basis, can be very effective (Gelzheiser, Meyers, & Pruzek, 1992).

For such instruction to work, it is essential that it truly be targeted and based on student learning data. This kind of teaching must be well planned and carefully coordinated with the instruction provided by the classroom teacher. Speculation about the failure of many pull-out programs suggests that one reason why things haven't always worked well is a lack of sufficient coordination (Allington, 1994; Davis & Wilson, 1999). If the classroom teacher and the reading teacher use separate curricula and separate materials, the extra teaching is unlikely to help the struggling students learn what they need to do well in the classroom. Of course, if the reading teacher is coming into the classroom, the need for coordination becomes even greater in order to avoid confusion.

Push-in services may take two different forms. One is to have the reading teacher sit with one or more students during lessons delivered by the classroom teacher, to individually guide them to better understand and gain from the instruction being provided to all the students. Another possibility is for the reading teacher to work separately with one or more students in need, providing intensive reteaching of the lessons on which the students are struggling.

In many schools, pull-out programs are preferred. In these efforts the students who have been identified as being in need of extra help travel from their classroom to another place within the school where the reading teacher plies his or her trade. These kinds of programs offer the reading teacher greater opportunity for flexibility in providing for students' needs and allow for the combination of students with similar needs from different classrooms. Of course, sometimes teachers don't work well together collaboratively, and this problem can be minimized by having the classroom teacher and the reading teacher working within separate facilities. Finally, in some cases students slip so far behind that the instructional assistance doesn't match well with the classroom instruction, so a pull-out situation can make it easier to provide instruction that closely matches student need.

Great care is needed to ensure that the intervention instruction, no matter how it is delivered, will be sufficient to improve students' reading skills and to provide a sufficient test of student responsiveness to intervention. The importance of coordination and collaboration between the classroom program and the extra instruction has already been noted, as has the need to use student data in targeting instruction, monitoring success, and guiding teaching. There are four additional key elements to making these intervention programs successful.

INCREASED AMOUNT OF TEACHING. One of the most important goals of a reading intervention implementation is that it provides additional instruction to the students (Gest & Gest, 2005; Linan-Thompson & Hickman-Davis, 2002). In the best of circumstances, this means that the help the reading teacher is giving should be coordinated in such a way so that it is extra teaching rather than replacement teaching. This might mean a school must schedule the teaching of reading at different times of the day for students at different grade levels or in different parts of the building. For instance, the primary-grade teachers might agree to teach reading in the morning, opening up the afternoons for extra instruction with the reading teacher, while the upper-grade teachers might agree to a reverse schedule. Too often the help that reading teachers provide is not managed in this manner, and so it replaces classroom instruction entirely or partially rather than supplementing it. In some cases, the lack of a clear scheduling plan actually leads to a reduction in teaching for the target students rather than an increase. For instance, let's say a classroom teacher teaches reading from 9:00 a.m. until 11:00 a.m. The reading teacher offers to give 30 minutes of extra help to three of the students in this class at 9:30. Often the classroom teacher will then not have these students participate in the first part of the class lesson, because they won't be able to finish, and additional time can be lost during the classroom transfer itself. Of course, increases in available instructional time can be accomplished by scheduling some of these services beyond the school day or school year.

TARGETED TEACHING. Another way the reading teacher can increase the chances of learning success is by making certain that the instructional help is well targeted on a student's greatest learning needs. In the regular classroom, a teacher has to try to teach all of the key skills and abilities commensurate with reading at the levels being taught. Because of the range of abilities and levels likely in a regular classroom, the teacher has to provide a thorough coverage of reading. This same kind of balanced approach is possible in a reading intervention, and such efforts have been effective (Manset-Williamson & Nelson, 2005). In a special reading class, however, the teacher can emphasize whatever part of the process a particular group of students is struggling with most (Fisher & Blachowicz, 2005). So if there are some kids who, despite receiving fluency help in the classroom, are still struggling, extra fluency instruction could be provided. Research has demonstrated that such targeted instruction in phonemic awareness, phonics, oral reading fluency, reading comprehension, or vocabulary—when added to a comprehensive course of instruction—can have a positive impact on reading achievement, both in the individual skill and in more generalized measures of literacy, too (NICHD, 2000).

In some cases, students lag behind in several skills simultaneously, but even in these instances it is possible that the reading teacher can offer the greatest assistance by targeting his or her efforts based on the student's relative pattern of performance. First-grade readers have to make clear gains in both decoding and fluency, but if students at this level are falling behind in both areas it is most immediately important to close the decoding gap and to target the extra instruction accordingly. Reading instruction that carefully prioritizes student needs and then changes these priorities on the basis of student learning progress is more likely to be helpful.

ADJUSTMENT OF INSTRUCTIONAL LEVEL. Another way the reading teacher can improve upon the classroom instruction is to vary the level of the teaching. When students are matched with materials that are too hard for them, it is difficult for students to make maximum progress (Faulkner & Levy, 1994; Hiebert, 2005; Morgan, Wilcox, & Eldredge, 2000; O'Connor et al., 2002; Shanahan, 1983). Classroom teachers can vary text levels to some extent, but it is often the case that students—especially struggling students—spend at least part of their instructional time working with materials from which they cannot make maximum gains because of the level of the material. In a special teaching situation, especially one that is meant to evaluate the students' responsiveness to teaching, it is imperative that text be better matched to student needs.

INTENSITY OF INSTRUCTION. Finally, reading teachers should make sure to boost the intensity of instruction. In classroom teaching, most of the time must be spent in whole-class or small-group teaching. One way of increasing learning is to make the size of the group small enough that student attention is captured as fully as possible and student engagement and responsiveness grow (Shanahan, 1998; Vaughn, Linan-Thompson, Kouzekanani, et al., 2003). When a kindergarten teacher is working with children on phonemic awareness, it is possible for students not to grasp the point of the lesson simply because of their inattention. However, when a reading teacher sits down with three kindergartners to provide such teaching, all of the those students will likely be able to see the teacher's lips and to hear the sounds more distinctly because of the reduction in distractions and interference. Students in such situations should be expected to respond more often than would be possible in a larger group situation, and reading teachers must take care to ensure that their lessons—usually delivered in advantaged situations in comparison to the regular classroom—make use of this added resource. Similarly, such small-group teaching increases the possibility of the teacher noticing any confusion or lack of understanding and to correct it immediately (again, something much harder for a classroom teacher to do).

This kind of special reading instruction can be delivered in a small group or even on a one-to-one basis. In any case, the degree to which the intensity of instruction can be increased has to be balanced with the need being addressed. It is not always necessary to teach the same way all the time. For example, one-to-one help for a student makes greater sense when something new is being taught (like a comprehension strategy, for instance), and group work makes greater sense once that strategy is understood and the student needs to practice and refine it in order to accomplish mastery.

Of course, there is no question that students benefit most when they receive help from a well-prepared and knowledgeable teacher, and it would be ideal if we could provide such teachers to all struggling students. Unfortunately, the reading case loads are inordinately extensive at some schools and the ability of a reading teacher to meet the needs of so many students would simply be impossible. However, research has shown that a skilled reading teacher can successfully organize, oversee, and guide the work of paraprofessionals and volunteers (Brown, Morris, & Fields, 2005; Morris, 2005). In such efforts, the direct instruction to students is being provided by the paraprofessionals, but within the planning and supervision of the reading teacher. It is not that the reading teacher delivers no direct instruction to students in these contexts, only that such teaching makes up a modest share of the extra help that the students get (but arranged so that the students get maximum benefit from the reading teacher's expertise and so that the paraprofessionals are not trying to make many professional judgments).

Summary

RTI efforts depend upon the expertise of many professionals within a school. This chapter has considered what role the reading teacher, coach, or specialist might play in this process. Generally, reading professionals can help improve classroom reading instruction through the professional development, coaching, or mentoring that they can offer to classroom teachers. Furthermore, reading teachers can provide high-quality reading interventions that raise reading achievement and provide an adequate test against which to evaluate a student's response to intervention. Such instruction needs to (1) coordinate carefully with classroom reading instruction, (2) be based on student performance data, (3) increase the amount of teaching students receive, (4) emphasize specific student learning needs, (5) be adjusted to student reading level, and (6) be of sufficient intensity that student learning results. Reading teachers are essential for an effective RTI program.

REFERENCES

Aaron, P.G. (1997). The impending demise of the discrepancy formula. *Review of Educational Research, 67*(4), 461–502.

Allington, R.L. (1994). What's special about special programs for children who find learning to read difficult? *Journal of Reading Behavior, 26*(1), 95–115.

Bean, R. (2003). *The reading specialist: Leadership for the classroom, school, and community.* New York: Guilford.

Blachman, B.A., Schatschneider, C., Fletcher, J.M., Francis, D.J., Clonan, S.M., Shaywitz, B.A., et al. (2004). Effects of intensive remediation for second and third graders and a 1-year follow-up. *Journal of Educational Psychology, 96*(3), 444–461.

Brown, K.J., Morris, D., & Fields, M. (2005). Intervention after grade 1: Serving increased numbers of struggling readers effectively. *Journal of Literacy Research, 37*(1), 61–94.

Davis, M.M., & Wilson, E.K. (1999). A Title I teacher's beliefs, decision-making, and instruction at the third and seventh grade levels. *Reading Research and Instruction, 38*(4), 289–300.

Dole, J.A., Liang, L.A., Watkins, N.M., & Wiggins, C.M. (2006). The state of reading professionals in the United States. *The Reading Teacher, 60*(2), 194–199.

Faulkner, H.J., & Levy, B.A. (1994). How text difficulty and reader skill interact to produce differential reliance on word and content overlap in reading transfer. *Journal of Experimental Child Psychology, 58*(1), 1–24.

Fisher, P.J., & Blachowicz, C.L.Z. (2005). Vocabulary instruction in a remedial setting. *Reading & Writing Quarterly, 21*(3), 281–300.

Gelzheiser, L.M., Meyers, J., & Pruzek, R.M. (1992). Effects of pull-in and pull-out approaches to reading instruction for special education and remedial reading students. *Journal of Educational and Psychological Consultation, 3*(2), 133–149.

Gest, S.D., & Gest, J.M. (2005). Reading tutoring for students at academic and behavioral risk: Effects on time-on-task in the classroom. *Education and Treatment of Children, 28*(1), 25–47.

Hasbrouck, J., & Denton, C.A. (2005). *The reading coach: A how-to manual for success.* Longmont, CO: Sopris-West.

Hatcher, P.J., Hulme, C., Miles, J.N.V., Carroll, J.M., Hatcher, J., Gibbs, S., et al. (2006). Efficacy of small group reading intervention for beginning readers with reading-delay: A randomised controlled trial. *Journal of Child Psychology and Psychiatry, 47*(8), 820–827.

Hiebert, E.H. (2005). The effects of text difficulty on second graders' fluency development. *Reading Psychology, 26*(2), 183–209.

International Reading Association. (2000a). *Excellent reading teachers* (Position statement). Newark, DE: Author. Retrieved February 15, 2007, from www.reading.org/downloads/positions/ps1041_excellent.pdf

International Reading Association. (2000b). *Teaching all children to read: The roles of the reading specialist* (Position statement). Newark, DE: Author. Retrieved February 15, 2007, from www.reading.org/downloads/positions/ps1040_specialist.pdf

International Reading Association. (2003). *Standards for reading professionals.* Newark, DE: Author. Retrieved February 15, 2007, from www.reading.org/downloads/resources/545standards2003/index.html

International Reading Association. (2004). *The role and qualifications of the reading coach in the United States* (Position statement). Newark, DE: Author. Retrieved February 15, 2007, from www.reading.org/downloads/positions/ps1065 _reading_coach.pdf

Jarvis-Janik, M. (1993). *The effectiveness of ESEA Chapter I pull-out programs on reading achievement.* Washington, DC: U.S. Department of Education. (ERIC Document Reproduction Service No. ED364833)

Linan-Thompson, S., & Hickman-Davis, P. (2002). Supplemental reading instruction for students at risk for reading disabilities: Improve reading 30 minutes at a time. *Learning Disabilities: Research & Practice, 17*(4), 242–251.

Manset-Williamson, G., & Nelson, J.M. (2005). Balanced, strategic reading instruction for upper-elementary and middle school students with reading disabilities: A comparative study of two approaches. *Learning Disability Quarterly, 28*(1), 59–74.

Mathes, P.G., Denton, C.A., Fletcher, J.M., Anthony, J.L., Francis, D.J., & Schatschneider, C. (2005). The effects of theoretically different instruction and student characteristics on the skills of struggling readers. *Reading Research Quarterly, 40*(2), 148–182.

Morgan, A., Wilcox, B.R., & Eldredge, J.L. (2000). Effect of difficulty levels on second-grade delayed readers using dyad reading. *Journal of Educational Research, 94*(2), 113–119.

Morris, D. (2005). A Title I reading success story. *Reading Research and Instruction, 45*(1), 1–17.

National Association of State Directors of Special Education (NASDSE). (2005). *Response to intervention: Policy considerations and implementation.* Alexandria, VA: Author.

National Institute of Child Health and Human Development. (2000). *Report of the National Reading Panel. Teaching children to read: An evidence-based assessment of the scientific research literature on reading and its implications for reading instruction: Reports of the subgroups* (NIH Publication No. 00-4754). Washington, DC: U.S. Government Printing Office.

O'Connor, E.A., & Simic, O. (2002). The effect of reading recovery on special education referrals and placements. *Psychology in the Schools, 39*(6), 635–646.

O'Connor, R.E., Bell, K.M., Harty, K.R., Larkin, L.K., Sackor, S.M., & Zigmond, N. (2002). Teaching reading to poor readers in the intermediate grades: A comparison of text difficulty. *Journal of Educational Psychology, 94*(3), 474–485.

Shanahan, T. (1983). A critique of P.A. Killgallon's study: A study of relationships among certain pupil adjustments in reading situations. In L.M. Gentile, M.L. Kamil, & J.S. Blanchard (Eds.), *Reading research revisited* (pp. 577–582). Columbus, OH: Merrill.

Shanahan, T. (1998). On the effectiveness and limitations of tutoring in reading. *Review of Research in Education, 23*, 217–234.

Shanahan, T., & Barr, R. (1995). Reading Recovery: An independent evaluation of the effects of an early instructional intervention for at-risk learners. *Reading Research Quarterly, 30*(4), 958–996.

Swanson, H.L., & Hoskyn, M. (1998). Experimental intervention research on students with learning disabilities: A meta-analysis of treatment outcomes. *Review of Educational Research, 68*(3), 277–321.

Sykes, G. (1999). Teacher and student learning: Strengthening their connection. In L. Darling-Hammond & G. Sykes (Eds.), *Teaching as the learning profession: Handbook of policy and practice* (pp. 151–179). San Francisco: Jossey-Bass.

Toll, C.A. (2004). *The literacy coach's survival guide: Essential questions and practical answers.* Newark, DE: International Reading Association.

Vaughn, S., Linan–Thompson, S., & Hickman, P. (2003). Response to Instruction as a means of identifying students with reading/learning disabilities. *Exceptional Children, 69*(4), 391–409.

Vaughn, S., Linan–Thompson, S., Kouzekanani, K., Bryant, D.P., Dickson, S., & Blozis, S.A. (2003). Reading instruction grouping for students with reading difficulties. *Remedial and Special Education, 24*(5), 301–315.

Walpole, S., & McKenna, M. (2004). *The literacy coach's handbook: A guide to research-based practice.* New York: Guilford.

Wepner, S.B., Strickland, D.S., & Feeley, J.T. (2002). *The administration and supervision of reading programs* (3rd ed.). New York: Teachers College Press.

Author Index

Note. Page numbers followed by *f* or *t* indicate figures or tables, respectively.

Subject Index

Note. Page numbers followed by *f* or *t* indicate figures or tables, respectively.